D1208230

1108

$ 10⁰⁰
NC

PRESENTED TO

_____

BY

_____

DATE

_____

# Textual Consultants

## Dr. Gleason L. Archer

*Professor Emeritus*
*Old Testament and Semitic Languages*
Trinity Evangelical School
Deerfield, Illinois

## Dr. Tamara C. Eskenazi

*Associate Professor of Bible*
Hebrew Union College
Los Angeles, California

## Dr. George Mason

*Ph.D. in Systematic Theology*
Pastor, Wilshire Baptist Church
Dallas, Texas

## Sr. Patricia McDonald, S.H.C.J.

*Assistant Professor*
*Department of Theology*
Mount St. Mary's College
Emmitsburg, Maryland

# The Illustrated

# Children's
# Bible

PAINTINGS BY

## Bill Farnsworth

HARCOURT BRACE & COMPANY

SAN DIEGO   NEW YORK   LONDON

## A Note on the Text

For the content of *The Illustrated Children's Bible*, we have drawn on various traditional texts, especially the Authorized (King James) Version. We have modified the traditional wording as necessary to avoid the unnecessary use of old-fashioned or difficult terms. The sequence of our Old Testament follows the sequence of the books of the Bible. In our New Testament, the four Gospels have been combined to provide a narrative sequence for the life of Christ.

Four Biblical scholars (see Consultants on p. ii) read every line of the manuscript for this book. Their comments were carefully considered, and many changes were made in the final text based on their suggestions. At all times we endeavored to achieve a balance between the most current research and a traditional understanding of the Scriptures. Our goal is to provide a Bible that offers a simple reading level and yet remains faithful to the most scholarly translations.

We hope that this book will serve as an intermediate stage between Bible picture books without text and a complete Bible in a standard translation. Our editorial policies have been explicitly devised for the young reader, such as the use of large and readable type, the inclusion of illustrations to accompany the text, and the presentation of episodes in narrative form.

This is the Greatest Story Ever Told. We invite you to read it.

*The Publishers*

## A Note on the Paintings

In the paintings that I have created for this book, I have been inspired by the many famous artists throughout history who have depicted scenes from the Bible. I hope my own efforts have been faithful to the great tradition that they established. I wish to dedicate my work on this project to my father, John Farnsworth.

*Bill Farnsworth*

## Acknowledgments

General Editor & Art Director: Christopher Morris

Project Editor: Elinor Williams

Contributing Editor: Gail Rice

Designer: Trina Stahl

Editorial Assistant: Joseph Sheehan

Text and maps copyright © 1993 by Harcourt Brace & Company
Illustrations copyright © 1993 by Bill Farnsworth
The Old Testament portion of this work is also published separately as *The Illustrated Children's Old Testament*.

All rights reserved. No part of this publication may be reproduced or transmitted in any form or by any means, electronic or mechanical, including photocopy, recording, or any information storage and retrieval system, without permission in writing from the publisher.

Requests for permission to make copies of any part of the work should be mailed to: Permissions Department, Harcourt Brace & Company, 8th Floor, Orlando, Florida 32887.

Library of Congress Cataloging-in-Publication Data available upon request.

ISBN 0-15-232876-9

First edition

A B C D E

Printed in the United States of America

# Table of Contents

# Contents of The Old Testament

# Contents of The New Testament

# Paintings of the Old Testament

# THE CREATION

In the beginning God created the heavens and the earth.

And the earth was without form, and empty, and darkness was upon the face of the deep. And the spirit of God moved upon the face of the waters.

And God said, "Let there be light." And there was light.

And God saw the light, that it was good, and God divided the light from the darkness.

And God called the light Day, and the darkness God called Night. And the evening and the morning were one day.

And God said, "Let there be an expanse of sky in the midst of the waters. Let this expanse divide the waters above from the waters that are below."

And God made the expanse of sky, and divided the waters that were above from the waters that were below. And it was so.

And God called the expanse heaven. And the evening and the morning were a second day.

And God said, "Let the waters under the heavens be gathered together into one place, and let the dry land appear."

And God called the dry land Earth, and the gathering together of the waters God called the Seas. And God saw that it was good. And God said, "Let the earth bring forth grass, let the plants give seed, and let the trees bear fruit." And it was so.

And that was a third day.

And God said, "Let there be lights in the heavens to divide the day from the night, and let them be for signs, and for seasons, and for days, and years."

And God made two great lights: the greater light to rule the day, and the lesser light to rule the night. God made the stars also. And God set all these lights in the heavens to give light on the earth. And God saw that it was good.

And that was a fourth day.

And then God said, "Let the waters bring forth all the moving creatures that have life, and birds that may fly above the earth in the open sky."

And God created great sea monsters, and every living creature that moves in the sea, which the waters brought forth in great number, all of their kind. And God created every winged bird, all of their kind. And God saw that it was good.

And God blessed them, saying, "Be fruitful, and multiply, and fill the waters in the seas, and let birds multiply over the earth."

And that was a fifth day.

And God said, "Let the earth bring forth all living creatures, each of his own kind: cattle and animals of the field, and creeping things, and wild beasts of the forest." And it was so.

And so God made the animals of the earth, each of their own kind, and God saw that it was good.

And God said, "Let us make humans in our image, after our likeness. Let them rule over the fish of the sea, and the birds of the air, and over the animals of the field, and over all the earth, and over every creeping thing that crawls upon the earth."

And so God created human beings in his own image. He created them male and female. And God blessed them, and he said to them, "Be fruitful, and multiply, and restore the earth, and master it." And God saw everything that he had made, and God saw that it was very good.

And that was the sixth day.

Then the heavens and the earth were finished, and all the things that filled them. And on the seventh day God ended his work. Then God rested from all the work he had done.

And God blessed the seventh day, and made it holy, because on that day God rested.

GENESIS 1; 2:1–3

# THE GARDEN OF EDEN

These then are the generations of the heavens and the earth, from the day the Lord God made the world.

No plant of the field was yet in the earth, for the Lord God had not caused it to rain upon the earth, and there was no one to farm the land.

But there went up a mist from the earth, and watered the whole face of the ground.

So the Lord God formed a man out of the dust of the ground, and breathed into his nostrils the breath of life. And he became a living being.

And then the Lord God planted a garden in the east, in Eden. And in the garden, he made trees grow that were beautiful to see and that had fruit that was good to eat. In the middle of the garden, he put the tree of life, and the tree of the knowledge of good and evil.

The Lord God took the man and put him into the garden to work it and keep it. The Lord God commanded the man, saying, "You may eat freely of the fruit from every tree in the garden, except from the tree of the knowledge of good and evil. For on the day that you eat fruit from this tree, you shall surely die."

And then the Lord God said, "It is not good that the man should be alone; I will make him a companion." And then he brought every living creature to the man to see what he would call them. And the man gave names to the birds of the air, and to every beast of the field. But for Adam there was not a companion.

So the Lord God made Adam fall into a deep sleep, and as he slept, the Lord God took one of his ribs, and closed up the flesh. From the rib, which the Lord God took from the man, he made a woman, and brought her to the man.

And Adam said, "This at last is bone of my bones, and flesh of my flesh. She shall be called Woman."

Therefore, a man shall leave his father and his mother, and shall cleave to his wife; and they shall be one flesh. And the man and the woman were both naked, and they were not ashamed.

GENESIS 2:4–25

# THE FORBIDDEN FRUIT

The serpent was more clever than any beast of the field that the Lord God had made. He said to the woman, "Has God said that you shall not eat from every tree of the garden?"

The woman said, "We may eat the fruit of the trees of the garden, but not from the one tree that is in the middle of the garden. For God has said: 'You shall not eat from it, nor touch it, or you will die.'"

But the serpent said, "Surely you will not die, for God knows that on the day you eat from the tree, your eyes shall be opened, and you shall be like gods, knowing good and evil."

And when the woman saw that the tree was good for food, and that it was beautiful, and that it was a tree to make one wise, she took its fruit, and she did eat. And she also gave the fruit to her husband, who was with her. And he did eat.

And then their eyes were opened, and they knew that they were naked. They sewed fig leaves together, and made themselves clothing.

Then they heard the voice of the Lord God, while they were walking in the garden in the cool of the day. And Adam and his wife hid themselves from the sight of the Lord among the trees of the garden.

The Lord God called to Adam, and said, "Where are you?"

And Adam said, "I heard your voice in the garden, and I was afraid, because I was naked. So I hid myself."

And the Lord God said, "Who told you that you were naked? Have you eaten of the tree from which I commanded you not to eat?"

Then the man said, "The woman whom you gave to be with me gave me fruit from the tree, and I did eat."

And the Lord God said to the woman, "What is this that you have done?"

And the woman said, "The serpent tricked me, and I did eat."

So the Lord God said to the serpent, "Because you have done this, you are more cursed than any beast of the field. You shall go on your belly, and you shall eat dust all the days of your life."

To the woman the Lord said, "I will greatly increase your sorrow and suffering in childbearing. In sorrow you will bring forth children."

And to Adam he said, "Because you listened to your wife and ate of the tree from which I commanded you not to eat, the ground is cursed for you. In sorrow you shall eat of it for all the days of your life. In the sweat of your brow you shall eat bread until you return to the ground. For out of the ground you were taken: dust you are, and to dust you shall return."

Then the Lord God made coats of skins to clothe Adam and his wife. And he said, "The man has become as one of us, to know good and evil. Now, he might put forth his hand and also take fruit from the tree of life, and eat, and so live forever."

Therefore the Lord God sent Adam and Eve forth from the garden of Eden. East of the garden, he placed angels and a flaming sword that turned every way, to guard the tree of life.

GENESIS 3

# CAIN AND ABEL

Adam called his wife Eve, because she was the mother of all living. Adam and Eve had a son, Cain. And Eve said, "I have gotten a man from the Lord."

Then Eve gave birth to Cain's brother, Abel. Abel became a keeper of sheep, and Cain was a farmer who worked the land.

In time it came to pass that Cain brought an offering of the fruit of the ground to the Lord. And Abel also brought the most prized of his flock. The Lord respected Abel and his offering. But the Lord did not respect Cain and his offering.

Cain was very angry, and his face showed his unhappiness. Then the Lord said to him, "Why are you angry, and why do you look so unhappy? If you do well, will you not be accepted? If you do not do well, sin lies in wait at your door. But you must rule over it."

Cain talked with Abel his brother, and it came to pass, when they were in the field, that Cain rose up against Abel, and killed him.

And the Lord said to Cain, "Where is Abel your brother?"

Cain answered, "I do not know. Am I my brother's keeper?"

And the Lord said, "What have you done? The voice of your brother's blood cries out to me from the ground. Now you are cursed from the earth, which has opened its mouth to receive your brother's blood from your hand. When you plant in the ground, it shall no longer give its fruit for you. You shall be a fugitive and a wanderer on the earth."

Cain cried to the Lord, "My punishment is greater than I can bear. You have driven me out this day from the face of the earth. I shall be hidden from your sight; and I shall be a fugitive and a wanderer. It shall come to pass that anyone who finds me shall kill me."

And so the Lord said to him, "Whoever should kill Cain, I shall take revenge on him seven times over." Then the Lord set a mark upon Cain, so that anyone finding him would not kill him.

And Cain went out from the sight of the Lord, and lived in the land of Nod, to the east of Eden.

Genesis 4:1–16

# THE LORD SPEAKS TO NOAH

And then it came to pass, that people began to multiply on the face of the earth, and daughters were born to them.

Then the sons of God saw that the daughters of mankind were pleasing to the eye, and they took as wives whichever ones they chose.

And the Lord said, "My spirit shall not always contend in man, because he is flesh. Therefore the days of his life shall be one hundred and twenty years."

There were giants on the earth in those days, and also after that. When the sons of God joined with the daughters of men and had children with them, these same children became mighty men, the famous ones of old.

And God saw that the wickedness of man was great on the earth, and that every imagination of the thoughts of his heart was continually evil. And the Lord regretted that he had made man on the earth, and it brought sadness to the Lord in his heart.

Then the Lord said, "I will destroy man whom I have created from the face of the earth; both man and beast, and also the creeping things, and the birds of the air; for I am sorry that I have made them."

But Noah found grace in the eyes of the Lord. Noah was a just man and was perfect in his time, and he walked with God. Noah was the son of Lamech, and the grandson of Methuselah. And Noah had three sons: Shem, Ham, and Japheth.

The earth was sinful in the eyes of God, and it was filled with violence. And God looked upon the earth, and saw that it was evil, for all flesh had corrupted his way upon the earth.

And God said to Noah, "The end of all living things is now at hand, for the earth is filled with violence, and I will destroy all the creatures that live on it."

GENESIS 6:1–13

# NOAH AND THE ARK

God said to Noah, "Make me an ark, a huge boat, of cypress wood. Make many rooms in the ark, and cover the ark with tar both inside and out.

"You shall make it in this way: The ark shall be 300 cubits long, 50 cubits wide, and 30 cubits high. You shall make an opening around the top of the ark. Make it one cubit wide. You shall set a door in the side. And the ark shall have lower, second, and third decks.

"And behold, I will bring a flood of waters upon the earth, to destroy all flesh, all things that contain the breath of life, from under heaven; and everything that is in the earth shall die.

"But I will make a covenant, a solemn promise to you. You and all your family will come into the ark, for I have seen that you are an honorable man in this generation. By this covenant, you shall come into the ark, you, and your sons, and your wife, and your sons' wives with you."

This Noah did, according to all that God commanded him.

Then the Lord said, "Bring with you into the ark two of every sort of every living thing, to keep them alive. And they shall be male and female. Gather also all food that is eaten, and take it into the ark for you and for them.

"Take seven pairs of every clean beast, a male and female of each, and two each of all beasts that are wild, the male and the female. Take seven pairs of all the birds of the air, the male and the female. Do this in order to keep them alive on the face of the earth.

"Seven days from now, I will make it rain upon the earth for forty days and forty nights. And every living thing that I have made I will destroy from the face of the earth."

And Noah did all that the Lord commanded him.

GENESIS 6:14–22; 7:1–5

Then Noah went into the ark, and his sons, and his wife, and his sons' wives went into the ark with him. Clean beasts, and beasts that were not clean, and birds, and everything that creeps upon the earth went, two by two, into the ark, the male and the female, as God had commanded Noah.

And it came to pass after seven days, that the waters of the flood were upon the earth. On the seventeenth day of the second month, all the fountains of the great deep were broken, and the windows of heaven were opened. And the rain was upon the earth for forty days and forty nights.

The flood was forty days on the earth; and the waters increased greatly, and lifted the ark up above the earth. And the ark floated upon the face of the waters. Still the waters increased, and covered the high mountains. Every living thing on the face of the earth was destroyed. Only Noah remained alive, and those that were with him in the ark.

But God remembered Noah and every creature that was with him in the ark; and God made a wind pass over the earth, and the waters grew calm. Then the fountains of the deep and the windows of heaven were stopped, and the rain no longer came down from the sky.

On the seventeenth day of the seventh month, the ark rested upon the mountains of Ararat. And then the waters went down until the tops of the mountains were seen.

And then at the end of forty days, Noah opened the window of the ark and sent out a raven. It flew back and forth, until the waters had dried up from the earth.

Noah also sent out a dove to see if the waters had gone off from the face of the ground. But the dove found no place to rest her foot, and she returned. Noah put out his hand and took her into the ark.

And so Noah waited another seven days, and again he sent out the dove from the ark. The dove came to him in the evening, and in her mouth was an olive leaf. Then Noah knew the waters had gone down from off the earth.

And on the first day of the first month of the next year, Noah removed the covering of the ark, and he looked out. And, behold, the face of the ground was dry.

GENESIS 7:6–24; 8:1–13

# NOAH HEARS GOD'S PROMISE

On the twenty-seventh day of the second month, God said to Noah, "Go forth from the ark and bring every living thing with you, that they may be fruitful and multiply upon the earth." And Noah with his sons, his wife, and his sons' wives, and every beast, every creeping thing, and every bird, went out from the ark.

Noah built an altar to the Lord. He took one of every clean beast and one of every clean bird, and he made burnt offerings on the altar. And then the Lord smelled a sweet odor, and the Lord said in his heart, "I will not again curse the ground for man's sake; for man may be tempted by evil even from his youth. Neither will I again destroy every thing living, as I have done. While the earth remains, planting time and harvest, cold and heat, summer and winter, and day and night, shall go on without stopping."

And God spoke to Noah, saying to him, "I establish my covenant, a solemn promise, with you, and with your children after you; and with every living creature that is with you; never again shall all flesh be cut off by the waters of a flood; never shall there be a flood to destroy the earth."

Then God said, "This is my token of the covenant that I make between me and you and every living creature that is with you. I do set my rainbow in the cloud, and it shall be as a token of an agreement between me and the earth.

"It will come to pass, when I bring a cloud over the earth, that the rainbow shall be seen in the cloud, and I will remember my covenant and the waters shall no more become a flood to destroy all flesh."

And God said to Noah, "This is the token of the covenant that I have established between me and all living creatures that are upon the earth."

GENESIS 8:20–22; 9:1–17

# THE TOWER OF BABEL

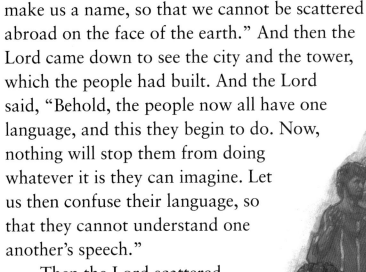

The whole earth once had one language and one speech. And as the people journeyed from the east, they found a plain in the land of Shinar, and so they settled there. There they said to one another, "Let us make bricks, and bake them hard. And here we will build us a city and a tower, whose top may reach up to the sky. And then we will make us a name, so that we cannot be scattered abroad on the face of the earth." And then the Lord came down to see the city and the tower, which the people had built. And the Lord said, "Behold, the people now all have one language, and this they begin to do. Now, nothing will stop them from doing whatever it is they can imagine. Let us then confuse their language, so that they cannot understand one another's speech."

Then the Lord scattered people from there all over the face of the earth. And they stopped building the city.

Therefore the city is called Babel, because it was there that the Lord confused the language of all the earth; and from there he did scatter the people all over the earth.

GENESIS 11:1–9

19

# ABRAHAM

Abraham was the son of Terah, and he was descended from Shem, the son of Noah. He lived in the land of Haran.

The Lord said to Abraham, "Go out of your country, from your birthplace and from your father's house, to a land that I will show you. And I will make a great nation of you, and I will bless you, and make your name great. And in you all families of the earth shall be blessed."

So Abraham took Sarah and Lot, his brother's son, and they went out into the land of Canaan. There the Lord appeared to Abraham and said, "To your descendants I will give this land." And Abraham built there an altar to the Lord, and he called upon the name of the Lord.

But there was a famine in Canaan, and Abraham went down to Egypt to live there, for the famine was terrible in the land. And Abraham said to Sarah his wife, "I know that you are a beautiful woman, and when the Egyptians see you, they will kill me but keep you alive. So, say that you are my sister, and I will live because of you."

And so it came about that the princes of Egypt saw Sarah and praised her before Pharaoh. And she was taken into Pharaoh's house. Pharaoh treated Abraham well for Sarah's sake, and gave him livestock and servants.

But the Lord sent great plagues upon Pharaoh and his household because of Sarah. And Pharaoh called Abraham to him, and said, "What have you done to me? Why did you say Sarah was your sister, so I would take her as my wife? Take your wife and go your way."

And Pharaoh sent Abraham away with his wife and all that he had. And Abraham, Sarah, and Lot took their possessions and traveled out of Egypt. They settled in a place between Bethel and Ai, where Abraham had built the altar to the Lord.

Genesis 12; 13:1–4

# ABRAHAM AND LOT

Abraham was very rich in cattle, in silver, and in gold. And Lot also had flocks, and herds, and tents. And the land was not able to support them both. There was fighting between the herdsmen of Abraham and the herdsmen of Lot.

Abraham said to Lot, "Let there be no fighting between us, for we are of one family. The whole land is before us. You choose the land to the left hand or to the right, and I will take the other."

Lot lifted up his eyes, and looked out over all the plain of Jordan. And he saw that the land was well watered everywhere. So Lot chose for himself all the plain of Jordan, and journeyed east. Then Abraham and Lot separated from one another, and Abraham stayed in the land of Canaan.

The Lord said to Abraham, "Lift up your eyes, and look from where you are northward, and southward, and eastward, and westward. All the land that you see there, I will give to you and your descendants forever."

GENESIS 13:5–15

# ABRAHAM AND SARAH

When Abraham was ninety-nine years old, the Lord came and said to him, "I am the Almighty God, and I will make my covenant with you. You will be the father of many nations. I will give to you, and to your descendants after you, the land of Canaan for an everlasting possession. And I will be their God."

Then the Lord appeared again to Abraham as he sat in the tent door in the heat of the day. And the Lord said, "I will surely return to you at this time next year; and Sarah your wife will have a son."

Sarah heard this from the tent door. Abraham and Sarah were old and far along in years, and Sarah had become too old to have a child.

Therefore Sarah laughed to herself, saying, "As old as I am, how is it that I will have a child?" But the Lord said to Abraham, "Why did Sarah laugh? Is anything too hard for the Lord? At the right time, I will return to you, and Sarah shall have a son."

GENESIS 17:1–8; 18:10–14

# SODOM AND GOMORRAH

Sodom and Gomorrah were cities on the plain of Jordan. The Lord said, "Because the sins of these cities are very great, I will go down to judge them."

Abraham asked the Lord, "Will you destroy the righteous with the wicked? If there are fifty who are innocent within the city, will you not forgive the place for them? Shall not the Judge of all the earth be just?"

And the Lord said, "If I find in Sodom fifty righteous men within the city, then I will spare all the place for their sake."

And then two angels came to Sodom, and said to Lot, "Bring your family out of this place, for the Lord has sent us to destroy it." The angels brought Lot out of the city, and one said to him, "Escape for your lives, and do not look behind you."

Then the Lord rained brimstone and fire out of heaven on Sodom and Gomorrah, and he destroyed the cities and all those within them. But Lot's wife looked behind her, and she was turned into a pillar of salt.

GENESIS 18:20–32; 19:20–26

# THE TEST FOR ABRAHAM

The Lord did as he had spoken, and Sarah bore Abraham a son in his old age. And Abraham called the son that was born to Sarah by the name of Isaac. And the child grew.

Then it came to pass that God said to Abraham, "Take your only son Isaac, whom you love, into the land of Moriah. Offer him there for a burnt sacrifice on one of the mountains that I shall show you."

And Abraham rose early in the morning, and saddled his donkey, and took two servants and Isaac his son, and he set out for the place that God had told him. And on the third day, Abraham lifted his eyes, and saw the place far off. He gave Isaac his son the wood to carry for the burnt offering, and he took glowing embers and a knife. And they went on together.

Isaac said to his father Abraham, "Here are the fire and the wood, but where is the lamb for the burnt offering?" And Abraham said, "God himself will provide a lamb for the burnt offering."

Then they came to the place that God had told Abraham of, and Abraham built an altar there. He bound Isaac his son and laid him on the wood of the altar. Then Abraham stretched out his hand, and took the knife to kill his son.

But the angel of the Lord called to Abraham from heaven, and said, "Do not lay your hand upon your son; for now I know that you fear God, seeing that you have not kept your only son from me."

Abraham looked up and saw a ram caught in the bushes behind him. And he sacrificed the ram instead of his son.

The angel of the Lord said, "Because you have not withheld your only son, I will bless you and multiply your descendants as the stars of the heaven and as the sand upon the seashore. And through your descendants, all the nations of the earth shall be blessed, because you have obeyed my voice."

Genesis 21:1–3; 22:1–18

# ISAAC AND REBEKAH

When Abraham was very old, he said to the eldest servant of his house, "Swear by the Lord that you will go to my country, to my relatives, and take a wife for my son Isaac." And he did so swear.

And so the servant took ten camels, and went to the city of Nahor in Mesopotamia. In the evening, he waited at a well outside the city as the women came to draw water. As he waited, Rebekah came to fill her pitcher at the well. She was the daughter of Bethuel, the son of Nahor, Abraham's brother. Rebekah was not married and was very beautiful.

The servant said to her, "May I drink a little water from your pitcher?" And Rebekah said, "Drink, my lord." When she had given him a drink, she said, "I will draw water for your camels also."

When the camels had finished drinking, the servant gave Rebekah a golden earring that weighed half a shekel, and two bracelets that weighed ten shekels. And he said to her, "Whose daughter are you? Is there room in your father's house for us to spend the night?"

Rebekah ran to tell her family of these things, and her brother Laban came to the servant and invited him to their home. They gave food and water to his camels, and set meat before him. But the servant said, "I will not eat until I have told you my errand." And he told them that he was Abraham's servant, and that he had come to find a wife for his master's son Isaac.

Then Laban and Bethuel said, "Take Rebekah, and go, and let her become your master's son's wife, as the Lord has said."

And they called Rebekah, and said, "Will you go with this man?" And she said, "I will go."

One evening, Isaac went out to the field, and he saw the camels were coming. When Rebekah saw Isaac, she got down from the camel, and said, "Who is that man who is coming to meet us?" And the servant said, "It is my master." So Rebekah covered her face with her veil.

Isaac brought Rebekah into his mother Sarah's tent; and Rebekah became his wife, and he loved her.

GENESIS 24

# JACOB AND ESAU

Isaac prayed to the Lord that Rebekah would have a child. And the Lord answered Isaac's prayer. Then Rebekah felt two children struggling together within her. Rebekah went to ask the Lord about this, and the Lord said to her, "You are carrying two nations: one shall be stronger than the other, and the elder shall serve the younger."

Rebekah's firstborn twin was red and hairy all over, and he was called Esau. His brother was born with his hand holding Esau's heel. He was called Jacob.

The boys grew. Esau became a skillful hunter, a man of the field. And Jacob was a quiet, thoughtful man, dwelling in tents. And Isaac loved Esau, for he liked to eat the venison that Esau brought. But Rebekah loved Jacob.

One day, Esau came from the field, and he was weak from hunger. He asked Jacob for some of the bean soup that he was cooking. Esau said to Jacob, "Feed me, I beg you, for I am faint with hunger." But Jacob said to Esau, "Sell me this day your birthright."

Esau said, "I am about to die of hunger. What good is this birthright to me?" So he sold his birthright to Jacob.

And then Jacob gave Esau bread and bean soup, and Esau did eat, and went on his way.

And that was how Esau gave up his birthright.

When Isaac was old, his eyes were so dim that he could not see. He called Esau to him and said, "Make me the tasty stew that I love, and my soul will bless you before I die."

But Rebekah heard what Isaac said to Esau, and she said to Jacob, "Do as I command you and fetch me two young goats. I will make the stew that your father loves, so you can take it to him, and he will bless you before his death."

Jacob said, "Esau is a hairy man; I am a smooth man. My father may feel me and curse me as a deceiver, not bless me." But he brought her the young goats. Rebekah put Esau's best clothes on Jacob, and she put the skins of the young goats on Jacob's hands and on his neck.

Jacob took the stew to his father and he said, "I am Esau, your firstborn." But Isaac said, "Come near that I may feel if you are Esau." Isaac felt him and said, "The voice is Jacob's voice, but the hands are the hands of Esau." But Isaac did not recognize Jacob, for his hands were hairy like Esau's hands. Isaac blessed Jacob, saying, "Let people serve you, and nations bow down to you. Be lord over your brothers."

When Esau returned, he cried to his father, "Bless me also." But Isaac answered, "Your brother has taken away your blessing. What can I do for you now, my son?" And Esau lifted up his voice and wept.

GENESIS 25, 27

# JACOB'S LADDER

Then Esau hated Jacob because of the stolen blessing. He said to himself, "The time of my father's death must be near. After the days of mourning for my father are over, then I will kill my brother Jacob."

Rebekah was told of these words of Esau, and she said to Jacob, "Your brother Esau plans to kill you. Go now to my brother Laban in Haran. Stay there for a time until your brother's anger is gone, and he forgets what you have done to him." She said to Isaac, "If Jacob takes a wife from this land of Canaan, what good will my life be to me?"

So Isaac blessed Jacob, and said, "Do not take a wife from Canaan, but go to Haran, and take a wife from the daughters of Laban, your mother's brother."

And so Jacob went toward Haran. Then he came upon a place where he spent the night. He took a stone from this place and he put it down for his pillow, and then lay down to sleep.

Jacob dreamed that a ladder was set upon the earth, with its top reaching to heaven. And the angels of God were going up and down on the ladder.

The Lord stood above it, and he said, "I am the Lord, the God of Abraham and of Isaac. This land on which you lie, I give to you and your descendants. I am with you and I will keep you wherever you go, and I will bring you back to this land."

GENESIS 27:41–46; 28:1–2, 10–15

30

# RACHEL AND LEAH

Jacob continued on with his journey, and then he came into Haran. There he stopped by a well where shepherds watered their flocks. As he spoke with the shepherds, Rachel came by with her father's sheep. Rachel was the daughter of Laban, his mother's brother. And when Jacob saw Rachel, he kissed her and wept loudly.

Then Jacob told Rachel that he was Rebekah's son, and she ran and told her father. Laban ran to meet Jacob, and embraced him, and brought him to his house. And so Jacob stayed with Laban for about one month.

Then Laban said to Jacob, "Though you are of my family, you should not work for nothing. What shall your wages be?"

Now Laban had two daughters: Leah the elder had tender eyes, but Rachel was beautiful. And Jacob loved Rachel. So he said, "I will serve you seven years, for Rachel your younger daughter."

And so Jacob worked seven years for Rachel, but they seemed only a few days to him, because of his love for her.

Then Jacob said to Laban, "Give me my wife, for the seven years have passed." And Laban gathered all the men of the place, and made a feast. In the evening, Laban took his daughter Leah and brought her to Jacob in bed.

And then in the morning, Jacob found that it was Leah, and not Rachel. He said to Laban, "What is this you have done to me? Did I not work for you for seven years for Rachel? Why then have you tricked me?"

Laban said to him, "It cannot be done in our land to give the younger daughter in marriage before the firstborn. But we will give you Rachel also, if you shall promise to serve me another seven years." So Jacob promised and was given Rachel. And he loved her more than Leah.

When the Lord saw that Leah was not loved, he blessed her with children. But Rachel had none. Leah had six sons, and then a daughter, Dinah.

But God finally remembered Rachel and heard her prayers. And so Rachel bore a son, and called him Joseph.

Jacob worked for yet another six years, and Laban gave him cattle. And Jacob had many cattle, and he became a man of great wealth. Then Jacob heard Laban's sons say, "Jacob has taken away all our father's wealth." And then Jacob saw in the face of Laban, that Laban was not as friendly to him as before.

And then the Lord said to Jacob, "Return to the land of your fathers, and to your family, and I will be with you."

So Jacob spoke first to Rachel and Leah. Then he set his sons and his wives upon camels, and he carried away all his cattle, and all his goods, to go to the land of Canaan.

And as Jacob went on his way, he sent messengers before him to tell his brother Esau in the land of Seir, that he was returning home and wished for his favor. But the messengers returned to Jacob, saying, "Your brother Esau comes to meet you, with four hundred men."

GENESIS 29–32

33

# JACOB AND THE ANGEL

Jacob was greatly afraid and distressed, and so he asked God to deliver him from the hand of his brother Esau. And Jacob sent ahead a present of goats, and sheep, and camels, and cattle to his brother.

That night, Jacob sent on his wives and his children, and he was left alone. In that place, a stranger wrestled with Jacob until daybreak. And when he saw that he could not defeat Jacob, he touched the hollow of Jacob's thigh. And the thigh was greatly strained. Then he said, "Let me go, for the day is breaking." But Jacob said, "I will not let you go unless you bless me."

And the man said to him, "What is your name?" And he said, "Jacob." Then the man said, "Your name shall no longer be Jacob, but Israel. For you have battled with God and with men, and have won." And he blessed Jacob there.

Then Jacob looked up and saw Esau and his four hundred men coming. And Jacob passed in front of his family, and bowed to the ground seven times, until he came near to his brother.

And Esau ran to meet Jacob, and embraced him, and kissed him. And they wept.

Then Esau said, "Why did you send me this present? I have enough, my brother. Keep what you have for yourself."

And Jacob said, "No, if I have found grace in your eyes, please accept my present, so I will know that you are pleased with me."

And Esau accepted the present. Then he returned that day to Seir, and Jacob journeyed on to the land of Canaan.

And it came to pass that Rachel gave birth to another son, and she died. Jacob called his son Benjamin.

And Jacob went to Isaac in Hebron, where the aged Isaac died; and his sons Esau and Jacob buried him.

GENESIS 32–33, 35

# THE COAT OF MANY COLORS

Jacob lived in the land of Canaan. And this is the story of the sons of Jacob, Joseph and his brothers.

Joseph, who was seventeen years old, was feeding the flock of sheep with his brothers. Now, Jacob loved Joseph more than all his other children, because he was the son of his old age. He made Joseph a coat of many colors.

When his brothers saw that their father loved Joseph the most, they hated Joseph and could not speak kindly to him.

Joseph dreamed a dream, and he told it to his brothers. He said to them, "I have dreamed that we were tying up bundles of grain in the field, and then my own bundle rose up and stood straight, and all your bundles stood around it and bowed down to mine."

Then his brothers said to him, "Will you then rule over us? Will we have to bow down to you?" And they hated him all the more for his dreams, and for his words.

One day Jacob called Joseph to him and said, "Go, I pray you. See whether all is well with your brothers, and with their flocks, and bring me word of them." So Joseph went into the fields, and he found his brothers in Dothan.

When the brothers saw Joseph coming from far off, they said to one another, "Look, here comes the boy who dreams." And they plotted against him. "Come, let us kill him," they said. "We will throw him into some pit, and say that an evil beast has eaten him. Then we shall see what will become of his dreams."

But Rueben, the oldest of the brothers, heard this. He said, "Let us not kill him. Do not shed his blood, but only throw him into this pit that is here in the wilderness, and do not lay your hand upon him." For Reuben meant to rescue Joseph from his brothers, and return him to his father.

So when Joseph came up to his brothers, they seized him and stripped off his coat of many colors. They took him and threw him into a dry pit. Then they sat down to eat.

Then Joseph's brothers looked up and saw a band of Ishmaelites coming with their camels, bearing goods to carry to Egypt. The brother named Judah said, "Come, let us sell him to the Ishmaelites, and let us bring no more harm to him. After all, he is our brother, and our own flesh and blood." And his brothers agreed.

As they were eating, some Midianite traders came by. They lifted Joseph up out of the pit and sold him to the Ishmaelites for twenty pieces of silver. When Reuben returned to the pit, he saw that Joseph was not there. He tore at his clothes, and he cried out to his brothers, "The boy is gone! And now, where will I go?"

The brothers took Joseph's coat of many colors. Then they killed a young goat, and they dipped the coat in its blood. Then they brought the bloody coat to their father. "We found this," they said. "Tell us if you know whether it is your son's coat or not?"

Jacob knew that it was Joseph's coat, and he said, "It is my son's coat. Some wild beast has eaten him. My son Joseph has been torn to pieces, there is no doubt."

Jacob wept, and put on funeral clothes, and he mourned for his son for many days.

Meanwhile, Joseph had been sold as a slave in Egypt. He was sold to Potiphar, the captain of the Pharaoh's guards.

GENESIS 37

38

# JOSEPH IN EGYPT

And Potiphar saw that the Lord was with Joseph, and he made Joseph the chief servant over his house, and he let Joseph manage all that he had. And it came to pass that the Lord blessed the Egyptian's house for Joseph's sake.

Now Joseph was a handsome man, and Potiphar's wife desired him. But Joseph refused her, saying, "My master has not kept anything in this house from me, but you, his wife. How can I do this great wrong, and commit a sin against God?"

Then Potiphar's wife grew angry. She told Potiphar that Joseph had mocked her, and turned and run away when she had cried out. When Joseph's master heard his wife's words, he became angry. And he had Joseph put into the prison where the king's prisoners were kept.

But the Lord was with Joseph and showed him mercy, and the keeper of the prison put Joseph in charge of the other prisoners.

GENESIS 39

39

# PHARAOH'S DREAMS

Once Pharaoh was angry with his chief butler and with his chief baker, and he put them in the place where Joseph was a prisoner.

There in prison, each one dreamed a dream. When Joseph came in to them in the morning, he asked, "Why do you look so sad today?"

And the chief butler said to Joseph, "I dreamed of a vine with three branches that blossomed and brought forth grapes. And I pressed the grapes into Pharaoh's cup, and gave the cup to Pharaoh."

Joseph said, "Within three days, Pharaoh will set you free, and you shall serve him as you did before. When you do, remember me. Show kindness, and speak of me to Pharaoh, that I may be set free."

Then the chief baker said, "I dreamed I had three baskets of bread on my head. In the top basket there were all kinds of baked goods for Pharaoh, but the birds ate them from the basket."

And Joseph said, "Within three days Pharaoh shall hang you on a tree, and the birds shall eat the flesh from you."

And in three days time all these things came to pass, just as Joseph had said they would happen. Yet the chief butler did not remember Joseph, but forgot him.

At the end of two full years, Pharaoh dreamed that he stood by the river, and seven cows, fat and healthy, came from the river and ate the grass. But then seven thin, sickly cows followed, and they ate the seven healthy cows. Then Pharaoh dreamed that seven ears of grain, plump and tasty, came up on one stalk. But seven thin and diseased ears swallowed up the good ears.

Pharaoh was troubled, and he told the wise men his dreams. But no one could tell him what they meant. Then Pharaoh's chief butler remembered Joseph, the Hebrew who could interpret dreams.

So Pharaoh called for Joseph and told him his dreams. And Joseph said, "God has shown Pharaoh what he is about to do. The seven good cows and the seven good ears are seven years of great plenty. The seven sickly cows and the seven diseased ears are seven years of famine that will follow. Let Pharaoh find a wise man and set him over the land of Egypt, to store food against the seven years of famine."

Then Pharaoh said to Joseph, "You shall be over my house, and all my people shall be ruled according to your word. Only I will be greater than you." And during the seven years of plenty, Joseph stored food in the cities. And Joseph had a wife, Asenath, and they had two sons: Manasseh and Ephraim.

GENESIS 40; 41:1–52

# JOSEPH AND HIS BROTHERS

After the seven years of plenty in the land of Egypt were ended, then the seven years of famine began. This was just as Joseph had said. The famine was over all the face of the earth, but there was food in Egypt. So all nations came to Joseph in Egypt to buy grain.

Now when Jacob saw that there was grain in Egypt, he said to his sons, "Go down to Egypt, and buy grain there, that we may live and not die."

So Joseph's ten brothers went down to buy grain in Egypt. But Jacob did not send Benjamin, Joseph's brother, with the others, for fear that some harm might come to him.

And Joseph's brothers came and bowed down before him with their faces to the ground. Joseph saw his brothers, and he knew them, but he did not make himself known to them.

Joseph spoke roughly to the brothers, saying to them, "Where do you come from?"

And they said, "We have come from the land of Canaan to buy food."

Then Joseph remembered the dreams that he had dreamed, and said, "You are spies; you come here to see the weaknesses of this land." And he put them in prison for three days.

On the third day, Joseph said, "If you are honest men, let one of you stay in prison while the rest take grain home. But bring your youngest brother to me, so I shall know that your words are true. Then you shall not die."

The brothers said one to another, "We are guilty because we saw the suffering of our brother Joseph's soul, and would not help him. Therefore, this trouble has come upon us."

And when Joseph heard them, he turned away and wept. Then he took Simeon and tied him up before their eyes. And the others loaded their donkeys with grain, and they returned to Jacob.

When Jacob heard their story, he said, "My son Benjamin shall not go with you, for his brother Joseph is dead. If any harm should come to Benjamin, I shall go down to my grave in sorrow."

But the famine was still great in the land of Canaan. And when they had eaten up all the grain that they had brought out of Egypt, Jacob said, "Go again, buy us a little food."

And Judah said, "The man did solemnly say that we shall not see his face again unless our brother is with us. If you will send Benjamin with us, then we will go down to Egypt. And if I do not bring him back to you, then I will bear the blame for this forever."

Then their father said, "If it must be so, do this: take the man a present of the best fruits in the land, a little balm, and a little honey, spices, myrrh, and nuts. Take your brother Benjamin also, and go again to him."

GENESIS 42; 43:1–14

# BENJAMIN IN EGYPT

The brothers went to Egypt, and Joseph's servant took them to his house. And when Joseph saw Benjamin, he hurried into his own room to weep, for he was deeply moved to see his brother.

They sat before him, and Joseph sent them food from his plate. To Benjamin, he gave five times as much as to any of the others. And they drank and were merry with him. Then Joseph told his servant to fill his brothers' sacks with grain and to put each man's money in the top of the sack. And in Benjamin's sack, he also put his own silver cup.

As soon as the morning was light, the brothers were sent on their way. When they were not far out of the city, Joseph's servant caught up with them, saying, "Why have you rewarded good with evil, and taken the cup from which my lord drinks?"

And they said, "God forbid that we should steal from your lord. Search, and let whoever took the cup die." When the cup was found in Benjamin's sack, the brothers tore their clothes in anguish, and they returned to the city.

When the brothers returned to the city, Joseph said to them, "Let the one in whose sack the cup was found remain here as my servant."

But Judah said, "Let me stay in my brother's place, for how shall I return to my father if Benjamin is not with me? Surely it will kill him."

Then Joseph wept loudly, and he said, "I am Joseph your brother, whom you sold into Egypt. God has sent me to you to save your lives.

"Hurry, and go to my father, and say to him, 'This is what your son Joseph wishes to tell you: Come to me now and live in the land of Goshen, you, and your children, and your children's children, and all that you have. There I will take care of you, for there are five years of famine yet to come.'"

And they did as Joseph said. And then Joseph went up to Goshen to meet Jacob his father. He presented himself to him, and he fell upon his neck, and he wept on his neck for a good while. And Jacob said, "Now let me die, since I have seen your face, and you are still alive."

But Jacob lived in the land of Egypt for seventeen years, and his family grew and multiplied there. And then when Jacob died, his sons carried his coffin into the land of Canaan and buried him there.

FROM GENESIS 43–45, 47, 50

# THE BIRTH OF MOSES

There rose up a new ruler of Egypt, who did not know of Joseph. He said to his people, "The people of Israel are stronger than we are. In time of war they might join with our enemies and fight against us. Come, let us deal cleverly with them, and get them out of our land."

Therefore the Egyptians put masters over the Israelites. They made their lives bitter with slavery, and with all kinds of hard work in the fields. But the more the children of Israel were made to suffer, the more they multiplied and grew. Then Pharaoh ordered all his people, "Every son of Israel that is born you shall throw into the river to drown, and every daughter you shall let live."

Now there was an Israelite of the house of Levi, who took as his wife a daughter of Levi. She had a baby son, and when she saw he was a healthy child, she hid him for three months.

When the mother could no longer hide her baby, she made him a basket of bulrushes. She sealed it with mud and tar, and she put the child in it. Then she laid the basket in the reeds by the river's edge.

The baby's sister stood far off, to watch what would happen to him. Then the daughter of Pharaoh came down to wash herself at the river. She and her servants walked along by the riverside. When she saw the basket among the reeds, she sent her servant to fetch it.

She opened the basket, and she saw that the baby was in it. The baby cried, and she felt sorry for him. She said, "This is one of the Hebrews' children."

Then the baby's sister came forward, and she said to Pharaoh's daughter, "Shall I go and call a nurse from the Hebrew women, one who will care for this child for you?"

Pharaoh's daughter said to her, "Go." And the girl went off and called the child's mother. Pharaoh's daughter said to the mother, "Take this child away, and nurse him for me, and I will pay you for it." Then the woman took the child away, and cared for him.

And when the child grew up, his mother brought him back to Pharaoh's daughter, and Pharaoh's daughter took him to become her son. And she said, "I will call his name 'Moses,' because I took him up out of the water."

EXODUS 1; 2:1–10

# THE BURNING BUSH

And it came to pass in those days, when Moses was grown, that he went out among his people, and he watched them at their hard labors. And he saw an Egyptian beating a Hebrew.

Then Moses looked this way and that way. And when he saw that no one was around, he killed the Egyptian, and hid him in the sand.

The next day Moses saw two Hebrews fighting, and he said to one of them, "Why do you hit your brother?"

And the man said, "Who made you a prince and a judge over us? Do you intend to kill me, as you killed that Egyptian?" Then Moses was afraid, and said to himself, "What I did has become known."

Now when Pharaoh heard of this thing, he meant to kill Moses. But Moses fled from Pharaoh, and went to live in the land of Midian.

There in Midian Moses lived with the priest Jethro, who gave him his daughter Zipporah. And she bore him a son, and Moses called his son Gershom.

In the process of time, the king of Egypt died, and the children of Israel groaned because of their slavery.

And then God heard their groaning, and God remembered his covenant with Abraham, with Isaac, and with Jacob.

Moses tended the flock of Jethro, and he led it to the mountain of God, to Horeb. And then the angel of the Lord appeared to Moses in a flame of fire out of the midst of a bush. Moses looked, and, behold, the bush was filled with fire, but the bush was not destroyed by the fire.

And God called to Moses out of the midst of the bush, "Moses, Moses." And Moses said, "Here I am."

And God said, "I am the God of your father, the God of Abraham, the God of Isaac, and the God of Jacob." And Moses hid his face, for he was afraid to look upon God.

EXODUS 2:11–25; 3:1–6

"They shall take the lamb's blood and smear it on the side posts and the upper doorpost of the houses. And they shall eat the flesh quickly that night, for it is the Lord's Passover." And the Lord said, "For I will pass through the land of Egypt this night, and I will kill all the firstborn in the land of Egypt, both man and beast."

And then the children of Israel went away, and they did as the Lord had commanded Moses and Aaron. And so it came to pass, that at midnight the Lord killed all the firstborn in the land of Egypt.

Then Pharaoh and all his servants rose up in the night. And there was a great cry in all of Egypt, for there was not a house without one that was dead. And Pharaoh called for Moses and Aaron by night, and he said, "Rise up, and go away from my people. Go now and serve the Lord. Take your flocks and your herds, and be gone."

And so it came to pass the same day, that the Lord did bring the children of Israel out of the land of Egypt.

EXODUS 11, 12

# THE PARTING OF THE SEA

The Lord went before the Israelites by day in a pillar of cloud to lead them. At night, he went in a pillar of fire to give them light. And they camped in the wilderness between Migdol and the sea.

And when Pharaoh was told the Israelites had fled, he said, "Why have we let Israel go from serving us?" Then he took all his chariots and horses, and his army, and he pursued the Israelites. And so the Egyptians overtook the Israelites camped by the sea.

As Pharaoh and the Egyptians drew near, the Israelites were afraid, and they said to Moses, "Why have you brought us out from Egypt to die in the wilderness?"

And Moses said to the people, "Do not be afraid, for the Lord will fight for you. Never again will you see the Egyptians."

And the Lord told Moses to lift up his rod, and stretch out his hand over the sea and divide it, so the children of Israel could cross over on dry ground.

Moses stretched out his hand over the sea, and the Lord made a strong east wind blow all through the night, dividing the waters. Then the children of Israel crossed on the dry ground in the middle of the sea. The waters formed a wall on their right hand, and on their left.

The Egyptians with all Pharaoh's horses, his chariots, and his horsemen followed the Israelites into the sea. Then the Lord told Moses to stretch out his hand over the sea so that the waters would come back upon the Egyptians. Moses stretched forth his hand. The waters returned and covered the army of Pharaoh, and not one of them remained alive.

Thus the Lord saved the children of Israel, and they saw the great work that the Lord had done for them. And Moses and the Israelites gave thanks to the Lord.

EXODUS 13:21; 14

# IN THE WILDERNESS

Moses brought Israel from the Red Sea, and the Israelites went out into the wilderness of Shur. They wandered for three days, but they found no water.

Then they came to Marah, but they could not drink the waters, because the waters were bitter. They complained, saying, "What shall we drink?"

Moses cried out to the Lord, and the Lord showed him a tree. When he threw it into the waters, the waters became sweet.

And then they came to Elim, where there were twelve wells of water, and seventy palm trees, and they camped there.

So they continued on their journey and came to the wilderness of Sin. And the children of Israel said to Moses and Aaron, "We would rather have died by the hand of the Lord in Egypt, for you have brought us out to this wilderness to die of hunger."

And then the Lord said to Moses, "Behold, I will rain bread from heaven for you, and each day the people shall go out and gather enough for that day.

"But on the sixth day, they shall gather twice as much as they gather on the other days."

And so it came to pass that in the evening quails came up and covered the camp. In the morning when the dew was gone, there lay a small round thing, as small as frost on the ground.

When the children of Israel saw it, they said, "What is it?"

And Moses said to them, "This is manna, the bread that the Lord has given you to eat. This is what he commands you: Gather enough to eat for one day, and let no one leave any till the morning."

But some did not listen, and left it until morning. And the manna smelled and was full of worms. And Moses was angry with them.

On the sixth day, they gathered twice as much manna, for the seventh day was the rest of the holy Sabbath. But some people went out on the seventh day to gather manna, and they found none.

The Lord said to Moses, "How long will you refuse to keep my commandments? The Lord has given you the Sabbath. This is why on the sixth day, he gives you enough bread for two days. Let no man go out of his place on the seventh day." So the people rested on that day.

And the children of Israel ate manna for forty years, until they came to the borders of the land of Canaan.

FROM EXODUS 15:22–27; 16:1–35

# THE TEN COMMANDMENTS

In the third month, the children of Israel came into the wilderness of Sinai, and camped at the foot of the mountain.

Moses went up the mountain, and God said, "Tell the children of Israel, if you will obey my voice, you shall be a treasure to me above all people, and a holy nation."

And Moses told the people God's words. And the people answered together, "All that the Lord has spoken, we will do."

And the Lord said to Moses, "I will come to you in a thick cloud, so that the people will hear when I speak with you, and will believe you forever."

And Moses brought the people to the mountain. And Mount Sinai was covered in smoke, because the Lord had come down upon it in fire. When the horn sounded long and became louder, Moses spoke. And God's voice answered him in thunder. God spoke all these words:

*I am the Lord thy God, who has brought thee out of the land of Egypt, out of the house of bondage.*

*Thou shalt have no other gods before me.*

*Thou shalt not make unto thee any graven image, or any likeness of anything that is in heaven above, or that is in the earth beneath. Thou shalt not bow down thyself to them, nor serve them: for I the Lord thy God am a jealous God.*

*Thou shalt not take the name of the Lord thy God in vain.*

*Remember the Sabbath day, to keep it holy.*

*Honor thy father and thy mother.*

*Thou shalt not kill.*

*Thou shalt not commit adultery.*

*Thou shalt not steal.*

*Thou shalt not bear false witness against thy neighbor.*

*Thou shalt not covet thy neighbor's house, thou shalt not covet thy neighbor's wife, nor his servants, nor his animals, nor anything that is thy neighbor's.*

EXODUS 19; 20:1–17

# ON THE MOUNTAINTOP

All the people heard the thunder, and they saw the lightning and the smoking mountain, and stood far off.

They said to Moses, "You speak with us and we will hear, but do not let God speak with us, or we may die."

But Moses said, "Do not be afraid. God has come to test you, so you will not sin." So he went near the thick darkness where God was.

The Lord said to Moses, "Say this to the children of Israel: 'You have seen for yourselves that I have talked with you from heaven.'"

And then God gave laws for the children of Israel to obey.

Moses told them the Lord's words. And with one voice, all the people answered, "All the words that the Lord has said, we will do."

Then the Lord said to Moses, "Come up the mountain, and I will give you stone tablets of the laws that I have written, so that you may teach them."

Moses went to the mountain. And the sight of the glory of the Lord was like a blazing fire in the eyes of the children of Israel.

Moses went into the midst of a cloud and went up the mountain. And he was up on the mountain for forty days and forty nights.

FROM EXODUS 20:18–22; 24:3, 12–18

# THE TABERNACLE

The Lord spoke to Moses, saying, "Speak to the people of Israel, and let them make me a sanctuary, so that I may dwell among them. They shall build the Tabernacle, according to the pattern I show you.

"You shall make an ark of acacia wood, and overlay it with pure gold, both inside and out. And you shall make upon it a crown of gold.

"And you shall make the altar for burnt offerings of acacia wood, with horns on each corner. The altar shall be overlaid with brass.

"Make a lampstand with six branches, and put on it seven lamps, that they may give light. And you shall command the children of Israel to bring you pure oil to keep the lamp burning always.

"And tell the children of Israel that they shall keep the Sabbath throughout the generations, for it is a sign between me and them forever.

"And I will dwell among the children of Israel, and I will be their God."

FROM EXODUS 25–31

# THE GOLDEN CALF

And when the people saw that Moses delayed so long to come down from the mountain, they got together and went to Aaron. They said, "Make us gods to lead us, for we do not know what has become of Moses."

And so Aaron said, "Take off your golden earrings, and bring them to me." So the people took off their earrings, and Aaron melted them down, and had a calf made from the gold. When Aaron saw the calf, he built an altar before it, and he said, "Tomorrow we shall make a feast to the Lord." The people rose early in the morning and made burnt offerings and peace offerings. Then they sat down to eat and drink, and they rose up to sing and dance.

And so the Lord said to Moses, "Go down from the mountain, because your people, that you brought out of Egypt, have become sinful. They have turned aside quickly from my commandments, and they are worshipping a golden calf."

And then the Lord said to Moses, "I have seen this people, and they are a stiff-necked people. Now therefore leave me alone, for my anger burns hot against them. I shall destroy them, and make a great nation of you."

But Moses pleaded with the Lord, saying, "Why are you angry against your people, that you brought out of Egypt? If you should destroy them now, the Egyptians will mock you. They will say you brought the people out only to kill them in the mountains, and remove them from the face of the earth.

"Remember Abraham, Isaac, and Jacob, your servants, whose children you swore you would multiply as the stars of heaven, and give the land to their descendants forever."

And the Lord repented of the evil which he had thought to do to his people.

Then Moses went down from the mountain. The two tablets with the writing of God engraved on both sides were in his hands.

But as soon as he came near the camp, he saw the calf and the dancing. And his anger became great. He threw the tablets from his hands and broke them at the foot of the mountain.

Then Moses took the calf which they had made, and he burned it and ground it to powder. He scattered it upon the water and made the children of Israel drink it.

And Moses said to Aaron, "What did this people do, that you have brought so great a sin upon them?"

And Aaron said, "Do not be angry, for you know that the people are always ready to do wrong."

Then Moses stood at the gate of the camp, and said, "Let whoever is on the Lord's side come to me." And all the sons of Levi gathered around him. And Moses said to them, "Each one take his sword and kill everyone who worshipped the golden calf, even if he is a brother or friend or neighbor."

They did as Moses said, and three thousand people died that day.

On the next day, Moses said to the people, "You have sinned a great sin. Now I will go up to the Lord, and perhaps he shall forgive you for your sin."

So Moses returned to the Lord, and asked him to forgive the great sin of the children of Israel.

The Lord said to Moses, "You and the people that you brought out of Egypt go forth to the land I swore to give to Abraham, to Isaac, and to Jacob. I will send an angel before you to a land flowing with milk and honey."

Then the Lord said to Moses, "Carve two tablets of stone, and I will write on them the words that were on the first tablets, which you broke."

Then Moses carved two tablets of stone, and went up on Mount Sinai. And the Lord descended and stood with him there. And Moses bowed his head and worshipped.

And Moses was with the Lord for forty days and forty nights. And he wrote the commandments on the tablets.

Then Moses came down from the mountain, and the skin on his face shone with the glory of God.

EXODUS 32–34

Then all the Midianites and Amalekites joined together to destroy the Israelites. But the spirit of the Lord came over Gideon, and he blew his trumpet made of a ram's horn, to call Israel to battle.

And the Lord said to Gideon, "There are too many people with you, and they will say that they have won the battle on their own without the Lord's help. Let anyone who is afraid return home." Then twenty-two thousand left, and only ten thousand remained.

But the Lord said, "There are still too many." So Gideon brought the people to the water to drink. The Lord chose those who put their hand to the water to drink, instead of bowing down. And of these there were three hundred men.

And Gideon divided the three hundred men into three companies, and each man had a trumpet, an empty pitcher, and a torch. They came to the Midianite camp in the middle of the night, and they blew the trumpets, and broke the pitchers, and held high the torches. The Midianites cried out in confusion and fear, and they ran away.

JUDGES 6–7

# SAMUEL IS CALLED

Now Hannah was the wife of a Levite named Elkanah, and Hannah had no children. And she wept, and she did not eat.

Then Hannah went to the temple at Shiloh, where the ark of the Lord was kept, and she made a promise, saying, "O Lord of hosts, if you will remember me and give me a man-child, I will give him to the Lord all the days of his life." And so then in time Hannah had a son, and she called him Samuel.

When the child was still very young, Hannah said to Elkanah, "I prayed for this child, and now the Lord has given him to me. Therefore I have lent him to the Lord for as long as he shall live." And they brought the child to the priest Eli at the temple in Shiloh, and Samuel served the Lord.

Each year Samuel's mother made him a little coat, and she brought it to him when she came to the temple with her husband to offer the yearly sacrifice.

And it came to pass that one night, when Samuel had lain down to sleep, the Lord called him. Samuel ran to Eli, and said, "Here I am, for you called me." And Eli said, "I did not call you; lie down again." And so Samuel went and lay down.

And the Lord called to him yet again, "Samuel." And Samuel got up and went to Eli, and said, "Here I am, for you did call me."

But Eli answered, "I did not call you, my son; lie down yet again."

And the Lord called Samuel a third time. And again he arose and went to Eli, and said, "Here I am, for you did call me."

Then Eli understood that the Lord had called the child, and he said to Samuel, "If he calls you again, say, 'Speak Lord, for your servant is listening.'"

Then the Lord came and called as before, "Samuel, Samuel." And Samuel answered, "Speak, for your servant is listening."

And then the Lord told Samuel that he would punish Eli and his descendants because Eli had not stopped his sons from doing evil.

In the morning, Eli said, "What did the Lord say to you? Do not hide it from me." So Samuel told him.

Then Eli said, "It is the Lord, let him do what seems good."

And Samuel grew, and the Lord was with him, and let none of his words fall to the ground. And all Israel, from Dan to Beersheba, knew that Samuel was a prophet of the Lord.

1 SAMUEL 1–3

# A KING FOR ISRAEL

And it came to pass when Samuel was old, that the people of Israel came to him, and said, "Find us a king to judge us like all the other nations." But this displeased Samuel, and so he prayed to the Lord. And the Lord said to Samuel, "Listen to the voice of the people, for they have rejected me. But tell them the ways in which a king would rule over them."

So Samuel said to the people, "A king will take your sons as horsemen for his chariots. He will make them plow his ground and reap his harvest, and make his weapons. And he will take your daughters for cooks and bakers. And he will take a tenth of all you have, and you shall become his servants. And you shall cry out on that day, but the Lord will not hear you."

Nevertheless the people said, "We will have a king over us like all the other nations, to judge us, and to lead us, and to fight our battles."

And so the Lord said to Samuel, "Listen to their voice, and find them a king."

1 SAMUEL 8

# SAUL AND SAMUEL

$N$ow there was a man of Benjamin, whose name was Kish, who had a son named Saul. There was not a man among the people of Israel more handsome than Saul, and he stood taller than all others. And the Lord told Samuel to choose Saul to be the first king of Israel.

So Saul took over the kingdom of Israel, and he fought against all his enemies on every side; against Moab, and against Ammon, and against Edom, and against the Philistines. And wherever Saul turned, he delivered Israel out of the hands of its enemies.

Samuel said to Saul, "The Lord remembers what the Amalekites did to Israel when they were coming out of Egypt. Now he wants you to go and completely destroy all that the Amalekites have. And do not spare a single man, woman, or child, or any of the animals."

And so then Saul called his men together, and they completely destroyed the Amalekites with the sword. But Saul and the people spared the king of the Amalekites and the best of all the animals.

The Lord told Samuel, "I am sorry that I made Saul the king, for he has turned his back on me and has not done my commandments."

Then Samuel got up early the next morning to meet Saul. He said to Samuel, "I have done what was commanded by the Lord." But Samuel said, "Then why do I hear the sounds of sheep and of oxen?"

Saul said, "They have brought them from the Amalekites, for the people spared the best of the sheep and oxen to sacrifice to the Lord. The rest we have completely destroyed."

And then Samuel said, "Did the Lord not send you to destroy the Amalekites? Why did you not listen to him, and do evil in his sight? It is better to obey the voice of the Lord than to make sacrifices to him."

Saul said, "I have sinned because I feared the people and listened to them. Now, I pray you, pardon my sin, so that I may worship the Lord." But Samuel said, "You have rejected the Lord, and the Lord has rejected you from being king of Israel."

Then as Samuel turned to leave, Saul took hold of his robe, and it tore. Samuel said to Saul, "The Lord has torn the kingdom of Israel from you on this day." So Samuel went to Ramah, and Saul went to his house. And the Lord repented that he had made Saul the king of Israel.

1 SAMUEL 9:1–2; 15

# THE SHEPHERD BOY

The Lord said to Samuel, "How long will you mourn for Saul? Go to Bethlehem, for I will provide a king from among Jesse's sons."

And so Samuel went to Bethlehem and he gathered the people to sacrifice to the Lord, and Jesse came with his sons. When Samuel saw Eliab, Jesse's first son, he said, "Surely the Lord will choose him."

But the Lord said, "Do not judge by his looks or by his height, for the Lord sees not as man sees. Man looks at the outward appearance, but the Lord looks at the heart."

And Jesse made seven of his sons pass before Samuel, and they were all tall and strong. But Samuel said to Jesse, "The Lord has not chosen these. Are all your sons here?"

And Jesse said, "The youngest stayed behind to tend the sheep."

Samuel said, "Send and fetch him." And Jesse sent, and brought David in. Now, David was handsome and had a fine appearance. And the Lord said, "Arise and anoint him, for this is the one."

Then Samuel took the horn of oil and anointed him, and the spirit of the Lord came upon David from that day forward.

Now the spirit of the Lord had left Saul, and an evil spirit from the Lord frightened him. And Saul's servants said to him, "Let us find you a skillful player on the harp, and when the evil spirit is on you, he shall play and you shall feel well."

And then Saul said, "Find a man that can play well, and bring him to me."

Then a young man said, "I have seen a son of Jesse who is skillful in playing, and who is a brave and handsome man." So Saul sent a message to Jesse, saying, "Send me your son David, who is with the sheep."

Then David came to Saul, and stood before him. And Saul loved him greatly, and made him his armor-bearer.

So it came to pass, when the evil spirit was on Saul, that David played the harp for him. And Saul felt well and the evil spirit left him.

1 SAMUEL 16

93

# DAVID AND GOLIATH

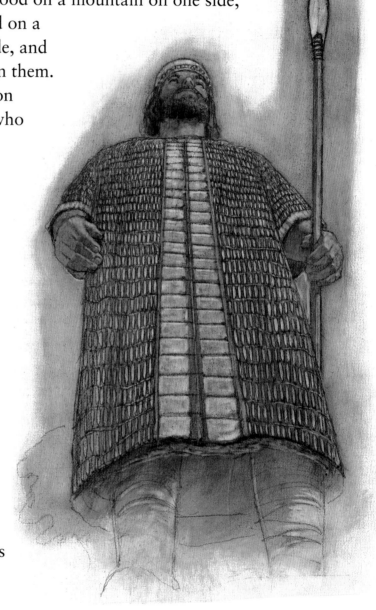

*T*he Philistines gathered together all their armies in battle, and were camped in Judah. Saul and all the men of Israel gathered together, and pitched their camp by the valley of Elah.

And the Philistines stood on a mountain on one side, and all the Israelites stood on a mountain on the other side, and there was a valley between them.

Then a huge champion named Goliath of Gath, who stood nearly ten feet tall, came out from the camp of the Philistines.

He had a helmet of brass upon his head, and he was armed with a coat of bronze. His spear was a huge beam, and its top was made of iron.

Goliath stood and cried out to the armies of Israel, "Why are all of you coming out to battle? Choose a man, and let him come down to me. If he is able to fight and kill me, then we Philistines will be your servants; but if I kill him, then you will be our servants."

94

And then the Philistine said, "I defy the armies of Israel today. Send a man out to me, so that we may fight each other." When Saul and the Israelites heard the words of the Philistine, they became very upset, and they were greatly afraid.

Now David had returned from Saul to feed his father's sheep at Bethlehem. And Jesse said to David his son, "Take this food to your brothers at the camp with Saul, and see if they are well."

David rose early in the morning and went, as his father had said. And David came to Saul's army and talked with his brothers. Goliath came up, and he spoke the same words. And David heard them.

And when all the men of Israel saw Goliath, they fled from him, and were greatly afraid. They said, "Have you seen this man who comes up to us? Surely he comes to defy Israel. And it shall be that the king will reward the man who kills him with great riches, and will give that man his daughter."

And then David said to the men that stood by him, "Who is this Philistine that he should defy the armies of God?" Then Eliab, David's eldest brother, heard what David said to the men. And Eliab was angry with David, and said, "Why did you come here? With whom have you left the sheep? You have come only to see the battle."

And David said, "What have I done now? May I not even speak?" And David turned away from his brother toward another and spoke in the same way.

David's words were repeated to Saul, and he sent for David. And David said to Saul, "Let no man's heart fail because of Goliath. I will go and fight with this Philistine."

But Saul said, "You cannot fight this Philistine, for you are but a boy and he is a man of war."

David said, "When I guarded my father's sheep, there came a lion and a bear, who took a lamb from the flock. And I went out after him, and hit him, and took the lamb out of his mouth. And when he rose against me, I caught him by his beard, and hit him, and killed him. I killed both the lion and the bear. This Philistine will be as one of them, because he has defied the armies of God."

David then said, "The Lord that saved me from the paw of the lion, and from the paw of the bear, he will also save me from the hand of this Philistine."

And Saul said, "Go, and the Lord be with you." Then he gave David his own armor, and he put a helmet of brass on David's head, and he armed him with a coat of bronze.

But David took off the armor, because he was not used to it. He took his staff in his hand. Then he chose five smooth stones out of the brook, and he put them in his shepherd's bag. His slingshot was in his hand, and he went nearer to the Philistine.

Then the Philistine came on and he came near David, with his shield-bearer in front of him. And when the Philistine saw David, he looked at him with scorn, for he was but a youth. The Philistine said to David, "Am I a dog, that you come to me with sticks?" Then he cursed David, and said, "Come to me, and I will give your flesh to the birds of the air, and to the beasts of the field."

And David said, "You come to me with a sword and a spear, and with a shield, but I come to you in the name of the Lord God of Israel, whom you have defied. Today the Lord will deliver you into my hands, and I will strike you, and take your head from you. I will give your dead body to the birds of the air and to the wild beasts of the earth, so the earth may know that there is a God of Israel. And all who are here will know that the Lord does not save with sword and spear, for the battle is the Lord's and he will give you into our hands."

And when the Philistine drew near to meet David, David ran out quickly to meet him. And David put his hand in his bag, and took out a stone, and threw it with his slingshot. The stone hit the Philistine so that it sunk into his forehead. And he fell on his face to the earth.

So David triumphed over the Philistine with a slingshot and a stone. When the Philistines saw that their champion was dead, they fled. And the men of Israel arose, and shouted, and chased after them as far as Gath and the gates of Ekron.

1 SAMUEL 17:1–52

# SAUL'S JEALOUSY

Saul took David that day, and would not let him return again to his father's house. David went wherever Saul sent him, and acted wisely. So Saul set him over the men of war.

When they returned from fighting the Philistines, the women of Israel came singing and dancing joyously to meet Saul. And they sang: "Saul has killed his thousands, and David his ten thousands." Saul was angered by these words, and he eyed David jealously from that day on.

The next day, the evil spirit from God came upon Saul, and David played the harp for him, as at other times.

There was a spear in Saul's hand. Saul threw the spear, thinking he would pin David to the wall. But twice David escaped from the spear.

Then Saul was afraid of David, because the Lord was with him. So he made David captain over a thousand men, and sent him away. And David won all his battles, because the Lord was with him. And all of Israel and Judah loved David.

So Saul went to the woman at Endor, and said, "Bring up for me the one I shall name."

Then the woman said, "Whose spirit shall I bring up?" And Saul said to her, "Bring me up Samuel." And so then Samuel rose up from the earth.

Saul saw that it was Samuel, and he bowed to the ground. Samuel said, "Why have you disturbed me?"

Saul answered, "I am greatly distressed, for the Philistines make war against me, and God has turned away and will not answer me."

Samuel said, "Why then do you ask me, since the Lord has now become your enemy? He has torn the kingdom from your hand and given it to David, because you did not obey him at Amalek.

"Tomorrow you and your sons shall be with me, and the Lord will deliver the army of Israel into the hand of the Philistines."

Then Saul was filled with fear, and he fell down full length upon the ground. There was no strength in him, for he had eaten nothing all day and all night. And so the woman brought food before Saul and his servants, and they did eat. Then they rose up, and went away.

FROM 1 SAMUEL 22; 25:1; 28:1–20

# DAVID BECOMES KING

Now the Philistines fought against Israel, and the men of Israel fled from before them. Many Israelites fell dead on Mount Gilboa. And the Philistines killed Jonathan, and Abinadab, and Malchishua, Saul's sons. Saul was badly wounded by arrows, and fell on his own sword, so that he would not die by the hand of his enemies.

When the men of Israel on the other side of the valley saw that Saul and his sons were dead, and that the Israelites were fleeing, they abandoned their cities and fled as well. And the Philistines came and lived in the cities.

When David heard that Saul and Jonathan had fallen, he tore his clothes and wept. And all the men that were with him mourned and wept.

And then David said, "The beauty of Israel is slain upon the high places! How are the mighty fallen! Tell it not in Gath; publish it not in Ashkelon; lest the daughters of the Philistines rejoice.

"Saul and Jonathan were lovely and pleasant in their lives, and in their death they are not divided. They were swifter than eagles, they were stronger than lions. How are the mighty fallen in the midst of the battle!"

And so the men of Judah came to Hebron. There they anointed David as king over Judah. Later all the tribes of Israel came to David in Hebron and anointed him king over Israel.

And so David ruled over the country for forty years. And during this reign, the Israelites defeated their enemies and rebuilt their cities.

David captured the city of Jerusalem, and he made it a holy city. And there he brought the ark of the covenant, in which the law of God was kept. And so Jerusalem became known as the City of David.

FROM 1 SAMUEL 31:1–4; 2 SAMUEL 1–3, 5, 6

# DAVID AND BATHSHEBA

And it came to pass one evening, that David arose from his bed and walked on the roof of his house. From the roof he saw a woman washing herself, and the woman was very beautiful to look upon.

So David asked about the woman. And someone said, "Is that not Bathsheba, the daughter of Eliam and the wife of Uriah the Hittite?"

David sent messengers to her, and she came to be with him. And then she returned to her house. In time, the woman sent a message to David, saying "I am with child."

So David sent for Uriah her husband. And when Uriah came to him, David asked him for a report on the army and the war. Then David said to Uriah, "Wait here today, and tomorrow I will let you return to the army."

In the morning, David wrote to Joab the captain of the army and sent the letter to him in the hand of Uriah. In the letter, David wrote, "Put Uriah in the very front of the hottest battle, and then retreat from him, so he will be struck down, and die."

And as Joab was attacking the city, he assigned Uriah to the place where he knew there were brave men. And so the brave men of the city came out and they fought with Joab's men, and Uriah the Hittite was killed.

When Bathsheba heard that Uriah her husband was dead, she mourned for him. And when the time of mourning was past, David sent for her and brought her to his house. Bathsheba became his wife, and she bore him a son. But the thing that David had done displeased the Lord.

And the Lord sent Nathan the prophet to David, and he said, "Why have you despised the commandment of the Lord? In secret, you have killed Uriah the Hittite and have taken his wife to be your wife."

And David said to Nathan, "I have sinned against the Lord."

Then Nathan said, "The Lord has put away your sin, so you shall not die for it. But with this deed, you have scorned the Lord, and the child that is born to you shall surely die."

And then the Lord struck the child that Bathsheba had borne to David, and the child was very sick. David prayed to God for the child, and he fasted, and lay all night upon the ground. But on the seventh day, the child died.

David arose from the ground, and washed himself, and went to worship in the house of the Lord. Then he came to his own house, and when the servants set bread before him, he did eat.

Then his servants said to him, "What is this that you do? You did fast and weep for the child while it was alive, but now that the child is dead, you rise and eat bread."

And David said, "While the child was alive, I fasted and wept, for I thought perhaps God would be gracious to me, and the child would live. But now that he is dead, why should I fast? Can I bring him back again?"

And David comforted Bathsheba his wife, and Bathsheba bore him another son, and he called him by the name Solomon. And the Lord loved Solomon.

FROM 2 SAMUEL 11:2–27; 12:9–24

# DAVID AND ABSALOM

Absalom, a son of David, had a beautiful sister, whose name was Tamar, and Amnon her half brother disgraced her. When King David heard about this, he was very angry.

After two years had passed, Absalom said to his servants, "Watch for a time when Amnon's heart is merry with wine, and then kill him. Do not be afraid." So Absalom's servants did as he had commanded. And then Absalom fled, and he went to live in Geshur for three years.

Then David sent for Absalom to return to Jerusalem. But he said, "Let him go to his own house, and not see my face." So Absalom lived for two years in Jerusalem, and did not see the king. And then David called for Absalom, and he came and bowed, and David kissed him.

But it came to pass that Absalom sent spies throughout Israel, saying, "As soon as you hear the sound of the trumpet, you will know that Absalom reigns in Hebron."

And a messenger came to David, and said to him, "The hearts of the men of Israel are with Absalom." Then the king and his followers fled to the wilderness between Jerusalem and the river Jordan.

As David made his way through the mountains, a man named Shimei cursed him and threw stones at him. David's servant said, "Why should this man curse the king? Let me go over and take off his head!" But David said, "Behold, even my own son wants to kill me. Let this man alone, and let him curse me."

The armies of David and Absalom met near the forest of Ephraim. David said to his men, "Deal gently with the young man Absalom, for my sake." And there was a great slaughter of twenty thousand men.

Absalom rode upon a mule, and the mule went under a great oak tree. Absalom's head was caught up in its branches, and the mule ran away. Then Joab took three spears in his hand, and he put them through the heart of Absalom, while he was still alive in the tree.

When the battle was over, the men ran to tell David that the Lord had delivered to them those who had lifted up their hand against the king. And David said, "Is Absalom safe?" And then a man said, "The Lord has avenged you today of all who rose up against you."

And again the king asked, "Is Absalom safe?" And the man answered, "May all the enemies of my lord the king be as that young man is."

Then the king went to his chamber, and wept. And he cried, "O my son Absalom, my son, my son Absalom! Would God I had died for you, O Absalom, my son, my son!"

FROM 2 SAMUEL 13–16, 18

# THE DEATH OF DAVID

When King David was very old, his son Adonijah said, "I will be king," for he was now the oldest, and a handsome man.

But Nathan the prophet spoke to Bathsheba, saying to her, "Have you not heard that Adonijah reigns in the land, and David does not know it? Go to David and ask him if he did not swear that Solomon should sit on his throne."

And as Bathsheba talked with the king, Nathan also came in. And he said, "My lord, have you said that Adonijah shall reign after you, and not told your servant?" Then David said, "I swear by the Lord God that Solomon shall sit on my throne."

And so Zadok the priest anointed Solomon. And the earth shook with the sound of the people rejoicing.

David commanded Solomon, saying to him, "Be strong and show yourself to be a man. Walk in the ways of the Lord your God, and keep his commandments, that you may do well in all that you do."

Then David slept with his fathers and was buried in Jerusalem, the city of David. And David had reigned over Israel for forty years; then Solomon sat upon the throne of David his father. And he established a mighty kingdom.

FROM 1 KINGS 1; 2:1, 10–12

# SOLOMON'S DREAM

Solomon took the daughter of Pharaoh king of Egypt as his wife, and he brought her into the city of David. Solomon loved the Lord, and he went to Gibeon to offer a thousand burnt offerings upon the altar there. In Gibeon the Lord appeared to Solomon in a dream, and God said, "Ask what I shall give you."

And Solomon said, "You have made me king in my father's place, and I am only a little child, who does not even know how to go out or come in. And I am in the midst of the people you have chosen, a great people, too many to be counted.

"Give me, therefore, an understanding heart to judge your people, that I may tell the difference between good and bad."

And this speech pleased the Lord, and so he said to Solomon, "Because you have not asked for a long life, or riches for yourself, or death for your enemies, I have done according to your words. I have given you a wise and an understanding heart. There were none like you before, and no other shall arise like you. And I have also given you that for which you did not ask, both riches and honor."

And Solomon awoke; and behold, it was all a dream.

1 Kings 3:1–15

111

# KING SOLOMON'S WISDOM

Once two women came to the court of King Solomon, and stood before him. "Oh, my king," said one woman, "I and this woman live in the same house. A child was born to me in that house. Then, three days later, another child was born to this woman.

"Only the two of us were in the house that night, and her baby died, because she lay on top of it as she slept. But then she got up at midnight, and took my living child from beside me, and put her own dead child in its place.

"When I awoke in the morning to nurse my child, I saw then that it was dead. But as I looked closely at it in the light, I knew that this was not my son, the one born to me." Then the second woman said, "No, no, the living one is my son! The dead one is her son!"

But the first woman answered back, "The dead one is yours! My son is the one who is alive!"

Solomon ruled in Jerusalem over all Israel for forty years. Then he died, and he was buried in the city of David his father. Rehoboam his son ruled in his place. The people protested against the heavy taxes and labor that Solomon had demanded from them, but Rehoboam would not lighten their loads. So the tribes of the north rebelled against the house of David. But the tribe of Judah still followed Rehoboam.

Now Rehoboam was not as wise as his father Solomon nor as brave as his grandfather David, and he could not win back the tribes of the north. They established a kingdom, and called it Israel. And their king was Jeroboam, the son of Solomon's servant. And the Lord was God over both of these kingdoms.

FROM 1 KINGS 11:1–13, 42–43; 12

# THE PROPHET ELIJAH

*T*hen the prophet Elijah came from Gilead and said to Ahab, the seventh king of Israel, "As the Lord God of Israel lives, there shall not be dew or rain these years." For King Ahab had done more evil in the eyes of the Lord than any of those before him. He had taken the Sidonian Jezebel as his wife, and built a temple to Baal. And there was no rain in Israel for three years.

Then Elijah went again to Ahab, and told him to gather all the people of Israel and the priests of Baal on Mount Carmel. And Elijah said to them, "If the Lord be God, follow him; but if Baal is god, then follow him." And so the priests of Baal prepared an offering, and called to Baal to turn it to flames. All day they cried out, but there was no answer.

Then Elijah prepared an offering to the Lord, and he said, "Lord God of Israel, let this people know that you are the Lord God." And the fire of the Lord fell, and it burned up the offering, and the wood, and the stones, and the dust.

The people fell on their faces, and cried, "The Lord is God." Then after Elijah had prayed for rain, the heavens became black with clouds and wind, and a great rain fell. The Lord told Elijah to choose Elisha, the son of Shaphat, to be prophet in his place. And Elijah found Elisha plowing in the field, and Elisha got up and went with Elijah.

Now when the Lord was about to take Elijah up to heaven, Elijah said to Elisha, "What shall I do for you, before I am taken from you?"

And Elisha said to him, "I pray you, let me inherit a double share of your spirit."

And Elijah said, "You have asked a hard thing. Nevertheless, if you see me when I am taken from you, it shall be so; but if you do not see me, it shall not be so."

But as they walked on and talked, a chariot of fire and horses of fire suddenly came between the two of them. And Elijah was taken up by a whirlwind into heaven.

And Elisha saw it, and he cried, "My father, my father; the chariot of Israel, and its horsemen!" And he saw Elijah no more.

And when the sons of the prophets saw Elisha, they said, "The spirit of Elijah does rest on Elisha," and they bowed to the ground before him.

FROM 1 KINGS 16, 17; 2 KINGS 2:1–15

121

# THE RETURN TO JERUSALEM

During the years after Elisha's death, the priests and the people of Israel sinned against the Lord and worshipped the gods of the heathen, and they polluted the house of the Lord in Jerusalem. And God sent his messengers, because he had mercy on his people. But the people mocked the messengers of God, and despised his words, until the anger of the Lord became so great that it could not be calmed.

Therefore the Lord brought the Chaldeans down upon them. They killed the young men, and had no mercy on the people. And they took to Babylon all the treasure of the house of God, and all the treasures of the king. The Chaldeans burned down the house of God, and they broke down the wall of Jerusalem. The people who had not been killed were taken to Babylon as slaves.

Then Cyrus the king of Persia captured Babylon. He sent an order throughout his kingdom, saying, "The Lord God of heaven has given me all the kingdoms of the earth, and he has commanded me to build him a house in Jerusalem in Judah. Therefore, let any among his people go up to Jerusalem, and the Lord his God be with him." And the tribes of Judah and Benjamin came out of exile, and went again to Jerusalem.

In the second year of the return to Jerusalem, the builders laid the foundation of the temple. And with trumpets and cymbals, they sang together and gave praise to the Lord.

But the enemies of the people of Judah and Benjamin set out to weaken them, and troubled them while they were building. They hired counsellors against the people, to frustrate their purpose. This went on through all the days of Cyrus, even up to the time of King Darius. But when Darius became king of Persia, he ordered that the house of God should be rebuilt, and all the treasures replaced there.

And when the temple was finished, the children of Israel dedicated it to God with joy and with sacrifices.

FROM 2 CHRONICLES 36:14–23; EZRA 1–10

# ESTHER BECOMES QUEEN

$N$ow it came to pass that King Ahasuerus of Persia decided to give a banquet in the garden of his palace in Shushan. He invited all the princes and nobles to show them the riches of his glorious kingdom and the honor of his majesty. And the banquet lasted for seven days.

On the seventh day, when the king was merry with wine, he commanded his servants to bring Vashti the queen before him, so the people and the princes could see how beautiful she was. But the queen refused to come at the king's command. The king was very angry and embarrassed, and he ruled that Vashti could never again come before him. He ordered his servants to find another queen better than she.

So the servants gathered all the young maidens of the kingdom in Shushan in the custody of the king's officer. And the maiden who pleased the king would become queen instead of Vashti.

Now in the palace of Shushan there lived a certain Jewish man by the name of Mordecai, whose ancestors had been carried away from Jerusalem. And Mordecai had become like a father to his cousin Esther, after her own parents had died. She was a young and beautiful woman.

It came to pass that Esther was taken to King Ahasuerus, and he loved her more than all other women. He set the royal crown upon her head and made her queen instead of Vashti. But Esther did not tell the king she was a Jew. Mordecai had warned her not to let this be known.

In those days, Mordecai often sat by the palace gates, and one day, he overheard two of the king's officers plotting to kill the king. And so Mordecai told Queen Esther, who warned the king of the plot. Both the men were hanged. And then, in the king's presence, this story was written in the book of the history of the kingdom.

ESTHER 1–2

# MORDECAI AND HAMAN

It came to pass that King Ahasuerus placed Haman above all the princes of the kingdom. All the king's servants had to bow down to him, but Mordecai did not bow down. Haman was very angry, and he decided to destroy all of Mordecai's people, the Jews, in the kingdom.

So he told King Ahasuerus, "There is a certain people who follow different laws and who do not obey you. If it so pleases you, have an order issued that they should be destroyed." And the king told Haman to do what seemed best. Then letters in the king's name were sent out, saying that all Jews should be killed, and their property taken away.

Mordecai told Queen Esther to beg the king to save her people. But Esther said, "If I go to the king's court without being called, I shall be put to death." And Mordecai said, "Speak now, or you too will be killed with all of your people. For who knows if you have not come to the kingdom for just such a time as this?"

So Esther went to the king's court. When the king saw her, he held out his golden scepter, and said, "What is your request, Queen Esther? For even if you ask for half of the kingdom, it shall be given to you."

Esther answered, "I would like you and Haman to come to a banquet that I have prepared." So the king and Haman dined with Esther, and after they had eaten, the king again asked what he could give her. And she said, "Come again tomorrow to dine with me, and I will tell you my request." And Haman was pleased because no other prince had been invited to the banquet but him. But he said to himself, "All this is as nothing so long as Mordecai the Jew will not bow down to me." So Haman had a gallows built on which to hang Mordecai.

That night the king had the book of the kingdom read to him. When the king heard again how Mordecai had once saved his life, he asked, "What honor has been given to Mordecai?" And the king's servants said, "Nothing has been given to him."

Then the king said to Haman, "What should be done for a man that the king wants to honor?" And Haman thought to himself, "Who else could the king wish to honor other than myself?" So he said, "Let this man wear the king's crown, and let him parade through the city on the king's horse." So the king said, "Hurry then, take my robes and the horse, and do this for Mordecai." And so Haman did as the king had ordered. But then he hurried off to his house, covering his head and weeping with sorrow.

That night the king and Haman again went to the banquet that Queen Esther had prepared. After they had eaten, she said, "Please, let my life and the lives of my people be spared, for we are to be destroyed." And the king asked, "Who dares to do this?" And Esther said, "The enemy is this wicked Haman."

So the king had Haman hanged on the gallows that he had built for Mordecai. And all the Jews were spared. And throughout the land, the Jews celebrated with joy and gladness.

ESTHER 1–9

127

# GOD'S SERVANT JOB

There was a man named Job in the land of Uz. He was a perfect and righteous man; he feared God and did not do evil.

Now, Job had seven sons and three daughters. He also had seven thousand sheep, and three thousand camels, and many oxen and asses, and a rich household. And so this man was the greatest of all the men of the east.

There was a day when the sons of God came to present themselves before the Lord, and Satan also came among them. And the Lord said to Satan, "Where have you come from?" And Satan answered, "From going to and fro on the earth, and from walking up and down on it."

Then the Lord said to Satan, "Have you considered my servant Job, for there is none like him on earth, a perfect and righteous man, one who fears God and does no evil?"

And Satan answered, "Job has every reason to love God. But if you take away all his riches, he will curse you to your face."

So the Lord said to Satan, "All that Job has is in your power. But do not touch Job himself."

Then one day a messenger came to Job and said, "The Sabeans have taken your oxen and asses, and they have killed your servants with the edge of the sword. Only I alone have escaped to tell you."

While he was still speaking, another messenger came to Job and said, "A fire has fallen from heaven, and has burned up all your sheep, and your servants. Only I alone have escaped to tell you."

While he was still speaking, another messenger came to Job and said, "The Chaldeans have carried away your camels, and they have killed your servants with the edge of the sword. Only I alone have escaped to tell you."

And while he was speaking, still another came, and he said, "A great wind came and knocked down the house in which your sons and daughters were eating and drinking. They are all dead. Only I alone have escaped to tell you."

Then Job arose, and tore his clothes, and fell to the ground and worshipped, saying, "Naked I came from my mother's body, and naked I shall return. The Lord gave, and the Lord has taken away. Blessed be the name of the Lord." And Job did not sin, nor did he curse God.

Once again there was a day when the sons of God came before the Lord, and Satan came among them. The Lord said to Satan, "Have you considered my servant Job? Although you moved me against him with no cause, he still holds fast to his honor and integrity."

And Satan answered, "A man will give everything he has for his life. If you put out your hand now, and touch his bone and his flesh, he will curse you to your face." And the Lord said, "He is in your power; only do not take his life."

So Satan caused Job to suffer from terrible sores, from the soles of his feet to the crown of his head. And Job sat down among the ashes and scraped himself with a piece of pottery. Then his wife said to him, "Do you still hold fast to your integrity? Curse God, and die."

But Job answered, "You speak foolishly. Shall we receive good at the hand of God, and not receive evil?" And in all this, Job did not sin with the words that came from his lips.

Three of Job's friends heard of his troubles, and came to comfort him. They sat with him, but did not speak, for they saw his grief was very great. At the end of seven days, Job cursed the day he was born. Then his friends tried to comfort him, and one of them said to him, "Suffering does not come up from the dust, nor does trouble sprout

from the ground. Man is born to trouble, as the sparks fly upward. But if I were in your place, I would seek God, and put my case before him. God does great things that cannot be understood, and miracles that cannot be counted."

And Job said, "Oh, that I knew where I might find God, so that I might put my case before him! I would know the words with which he would answer me, and understand what he would say."

Then the Lord answered Job out of the whirlwind, saying, "I will question you, and you shall answer me. Where were you when I laid the foundation of the earth? When the morning stars sang together, and all the sons of God shouted for joy? And who shut in the sea with doors when it burst forth? Have you commanded the morning, and caused the dawn to know its place? Have you seen the doors of the shadow of death? Have you seen the treasures of the snow, or of the hail? Do you know how the light is parted, that scatters the east wind upon the earth? Will you hunt prey for the lions or provide food for the raven? Have you given the horse strength? Does the hawk fly by your wisdom? He that finds fault with the Lord, let him answer."

Then Job answered the Lord, "I know you can do everything, and that no thought can be hidden from you. I spoke about what I did not understand, things too wonderful to know. I have heard of you by my ears, but now my eyes see you. Therefore I repent in dust and ashes."

And the Lord accepted Job's words, and he blessed the later life of Job even more than the beginning, for he gave Job twice as much as he had given him before. Seven more sons and three more daughters were born to Job. And he lived to be a very old man.

JOB 1–42

# from THE BOOK OF PSALMS

*O Lord our Lord, how excellent is thy name in all the earth!
who hast set thy glory above the heavens.*

*Out of the mouth of babes and sucklings hast thou ordained
strength because of thine enemies, that thou mightest still the
enemy and the avenger.*

*When I consider thy heavens, the work of thy fingers, the moon
and the stars, which thou has ordained;*

*What is man, that thou are mindful of him? and the son of
man, that thou visiteth him?*

*For thou has made him a little lower than the angels, and hast
crowned him with glory and honor.*

*Thou madest him to have dominion over the works of thy
hands: thou hast put all things under his feet:*

*All sheep and oxen, yea, and the beasts of the field;*

*The fowl of the air, and the fish of the sea, and whatsoever
passeth through the paths of the seas.*

*O Lord our Lord, how excellent is thy name in all the earth!*

PSALM 8

*Make a joyful noise unto the Lord, all ye lands.*

*Serve the Lord with gladness: come before his presence with
singing.*

*Know ye that the Lord he is God: it is he that hath made us,
and not we ourselves; we are his people, and the sheep of his
pasture.*

*Enter into his gates with thanksgiving, and into his courts with
praise: be thankful unto him, and bless his name.*

*For the Lord is good; his mercy is everlasting: and his truth
endureth to all generations.*

PSALM 100

*The Lord is my shepherd; I shall not want.*

*He maketh me to lie down in green pastures: he leadeth me beside the still waters.*

*He restoreth my soul: he leadeth me in the paths of righteousness for his name's sake.*

*Yea, though I walk through the valley of the shadow of death, I will fear no evil: for thou art with me; thy rod and thy staff they comfort me.*

*Thou preparest a table before me in the presence of mine enemies: thou anointest my head with oil; my cup runneth over.*

*Surely goodness and mercy shall follow me all the days of my life: and I will dwell in the house of the Lord forever.*

PSALM 23

*I will lift up mine eyes unto the hills, from whence cometh my help.*

*My help cometh from the Lord, which made heaven and earth.*

*He will not suffer thy foot to be moved; he that keepeth thee will not slumber.*

*Behold, he that keepeth Israel shall neither slumber nor sleep.*

*The Lord is thy keeper: the Lord is thy shade upon thy right hand.*

*The sun shall not smite thee by day, nor the moon by night.*

*The Lord shall preserve thee from all evil: he shall preserve thy soul.*

*The Lord shall preserve thy going out and thy coming in from this time forth, and even for evermore.*

PSALM 121

*By the rivers of Babylon, there we sat down, yea, we wept,*
*    when we remembered Zion.*
*We hanged our harps upon the willows in the midst thereof.*
*For there they that carried us away captive required of us a*
*    song; and they that wasted us required of us mirth, saying,*
*    "Sing us one of the songs of Zion."*
*How shall we sing the Lord's song in a strange land?*
*If I forget thee, O Jerusalem, let my right hand forget her*
*    cunning.*
*If I do not remember thee, let my tongue cleave to the roof of*
*    my mouth; if I prefer not Jerusalem above my chief joy.*
*Remember, O Lord, the children of Edom in the day of*
*    Jerusalem; who said, "Raze it, raze it, even to the foundation*
*    thereof."*
*O daughter of Babylon, who art to be destroyed; happy shall*
*    he be, that rewardeth thee as thou hast served us.*
*Happy shall he be, that taketh and dasheth thy little ones*
*    against the stones.*

PSALM 137

*The Lord reigneth, he is clothed with majesty; the Lord is*
*    clothed with strength, wherewith he hath girded himself: the*
*    world also is stabilized, that it cannot be moved.*
*Thy throne is established of old: thou art from everlasting.*
*The floods have lifted up, O Lord, the floods have lifted up*
*    their voice; the floods lift up their waves.*
*The Lord on high is mightier than the noise of many waters,*
*    yea, than the mighty waves of the sea.*
*Thy testimonies are very sure: holiness becometh thine house,*
*    O Lord, forever.*

PSALM 93

# FROM PROVERBS

*A wise son makes a glad father: but a foolish son is the heaviness of his mother.*

*The wicked flee when no man pursues: but the righteous are bold as a lion.*

*He that spares his rod hates his son: but he that loves him chastens him sometimes.*

*He that troubles his own house shall inherit the wind.*

*A soft answer turns away wrath.*

*Better is a dinner of herbs where love is, than a stalled ox and hatred therewith.*

*Pride goes before destruction, and a haughty spirit before a fall.*

*Even a fool, when he holds his peace, is counted wise.*

*A friend loves at all times, and a brother is born for adversity.*

*Better is a neighbor that is near than a brother far off.*

*A merry heart does good like a medicine: but a broken spirit dries the bones.*

*Even a child is known by his doings, whether his work be pure, and whether it be right.*

*A good name is rather to be chosen than great riches.*

*Train up a child in the way he should go; and when he is old, he will not depart from it.*

*The borrower is servant to the lender.*

*Riches certainly make themselves wings; they fly away as an eagle toward heaven.*

*Despise not your mother when she is old.*

*Let another man praise you, and not your own mouth.*

*Wealth makes many friends; but the poor is separated from his neighbor.*

*A false witness shall not be unpunished, and he that speaks lies shall not escape.*

# FROM ECCLESIASTES

*Vanity of vanities, says the Preacher, vanity of vanities; all is vanity.*

*What does a man gain from all the labor he takes under the sun? One generation passes away, and another generation comes: but the earth remains forever.*

*The sun also rises, and the sun goes down, and hastens to his place where he arose.*

*All the rivers run into the sea; yet the sea is not full; unto the place from whence the rivers come, there they return again.*

*All things are full of labor; man cannot utter it: the eye is not satisfied with seeing, nor the ear filled with hearing.*

*The thing that has been, it is that which shall be; and that which is done is that which shall be done: and there is no new thing under the sun.*

*For every thing there is a season, and a time for every purpose under heaven:*

*A time to be born, and a time to die; a time to plant, and a time to pluck up that which is planted;*

*A time to kill, and a time to heal; a time to break down, and a time to build up;*

*A time to weep, and a time to laugh; a time to mourn, and a time to dance;*

*A time to cast away stones, and a time to gather stones together; a time to embrace, and a time to refrain from embracing;*

*A time to get, and a time to lose; a time to keep, and a time to cast away;*

*A time to rend, and a time to sew; a time to keep silence, and a time to speak;*

*A time to love, and a time to hate; a time of war, and a time of peace.*

# FROM *THE SONG OF SONGS*

*I have compared you, O my love, to a company of horses in
  Pharaoh's chariots.
Your cheeks are comely with rows of jewels, your neck with
  chains of gold.
We will make you borders of gold with studs of silver.*

*I am the rose of Sharon, and the lily of the valleys.
As the lily among thorns, so is my love among the daughters.
As the apple tree among the trees of the wood, so is my beloved
  among the sons.*

*My beloved spoke, and said unto me, "Rise up, my love, my fair
  one, and come away.
For, lo, the winter is past, the rain is over and gone;
The flowers appear on the earth; the time of the singing of birds
  is come, and the voice of the turtle is heard in our land;
The fig tree puts forth her green figs, and the vines with the
  tender grape give a good smell. Arise, my love, my fair one,
  and come away."*

*Who is this that comes out of the wilderness like pillars of
  smoke, perfumed with myrrh and frankincense, with all
  powders of the merchant?*

*Awake, O north wind; and come, thou south; blow upon my
  garden, that the spices thereof may flow out. Let my beloved
  come into his garden, and eat his pleasant fruits.*

*Until the day break, and the shadows flee away, get me to the
  mountain of myrrh, and to the hill of frankincense.*

# FROM *THE BOOK OF ISAIAH*

"Come now, and let us reason together, " said the Lord: "For though your sins be scarlet, they shall be as white as snow; though they be red like crimson, they shall be as white as wool."

The Lord shall judge among the nations, and he shall rebuke many people. They shall beat their swords into plowshares, and their spears into pruning hooks: nation shall not lift up sword against nation, neither shall they learn war any more.

Holy, holy, holy, is the Lord of hosts: the earth is full of his glory.

Therefore the Lord himself shall give you a sign: Behold, a virgin shall be with child, and bear a son, and shall call his name Immanuel.

Butter and honey shall he eat, that he may know to refuse the evil, and choose the good.

For unto us a child is born, unto us a son is given: and the government shall be upon his shoulder: and his name shall be called Wonderful Counselor, Mighty God, Everlasting Father, Prince of Peace.

And there shall come forth a rod out of the stem of Jesse, and a branch shall grow out of his roots.

And the Spirit of the Lord shall rest upon him, the spirit of wisdom and of understanding, the spirit of counsel and of might, the spirit of knowledge and of the fear of the Lord.

The wolf also shall dwell with the lamb, and the leopard shall lie down with the kid, and the calf and the young lion and the fatling together. And a little child shall lead them.

And the cow and the bear shall feed; their young ones shall lie down together: and the lion shall eat straw like the ox.

And the suckling child shall play on the hole of the asp, and the weaned child shall put his hand on the den of the cockatrice.

They shall not hurt nor destroy in all my holy mountain: for the earth shall be full of the knowledge of the Lord, as the waters cover the sea.

A voice cries in the wilderness: "Prepare you the way of the Lord, make straight in the desert a highway for our God.

"Every valley shall be raised up, and every mountain and hill shall be made low; and the crooked shall be made straight, and the rough places made plain.

"And the glory of the Lord shall be revealed, and all who are flesh shall see it together: for the mouth of the Lord has spoken."

ISAIAH 1, 6, 7, 9, 11, 40

# KING NEBUCHADNEZZAR

In the third year of the reign of Jehoiakim, king of Judah, King Nebuchadnezzar of Babylon captured Jerusalem. He took some of the vessels of the house of God back to his land, to the house of his god.

King Nebuchadnezzar had certain of the Israelite children brought to his palace. These children were handsome, and skillful and clever, and were quick to understand. The king wanted the children to learn the ways and the language of the Babylonians, so they could serve him.

Now among those chosen from Judah were these four: Daniel, Hananiah, Mishael, and Azariah. They were given Babylonian names: Daniel was called Belteshazzar; and Hananiah was called Shadrach; Mishael was called Meshach; and Azariah was called Abednego.

Daniel and the others did not eat the king's rich food and wine, because it was against God's law. But they were more healthy than those who did, even though they lived on only vegetables and water.

God gave these young men knowledge and skill in all learning, and Daniel understood visions and dreams. The king spoke with them. And in all matters of wisdom and understanding, he found them ten times better than all the magicians and astrologers in his kingdom.

DANIEL 1:1–7, 17–20

# HANDWRITING ON THE WALL

King Belshazzar ruled Babylon after the death of his ancestor Nebuchadnezzar. One night King Belshazzar held a great banquet for one thousand of his lords, and he drank wine before the thousand.

While Belshazzar tasted the wine, he had brought to him the golden and silver vessels which Nebuchadnezzar had taken from the temple of the house of God, which was in Jerusalem. And when the vessels were brought in, the king and his guests did drink wine from them. As they drank the wine, they praised their gods of gold and silver, of bronze, iron, wood, and stone.

Then suddenly the fingers of a man's hand came forth and wrote on the wall of the banquet room. The king saw the hand as it wrote.

Then the king's face was changed, and his thoughts were troubled. His knees knocked against each other and his legs were weak. He cried out loud to bring in all his astrologers and soothsayers.

And the king spoke, and he said to these wise men of Babylon,

"Whoever can read this writing, and can show me the meaning of it, shall be dressed in scarlet, and have a chain of gold about his neck. And he shall be the third ruler in the kingdom."

Then all the king's wise men came in, but they could not read the writing, nor could they interpret it for the king.

And so King Belshazzar was very troubled. Now the queen mother spoke and said, "O king, do not let your thoughts trouble you, for there is a man in your kingdom, whose name is Daniel. Wisdom like the wisdom of the holy gods is found in him, and your ancestor King Nebuchadnezzar made him the master of all the magicians. This man can interpret dreams and solve problems."

Then Daniel was brought in, and Belshazzar said to him, "Are you Daniel, who was brought out of Jerusalem as a captive by my father the king? I have heard of you, and I have heard that the spirit of the gods is in you, and that light and understanding and excellent wisdom are found in you. If you can read the writing and can tell me what it means, you shall be clothed in scarlet, and have a chain of gold around your neck, and you shall be the third ruler in the kingdom."

And Daniel said, "Let your gifts be given to another, but I will read the writing and interpret it for you. O, Belshazzar, you have not humbled your heart, but have lifted yourself against the Lord. You have brought the vessels from his house, and you and your guests have drunk wine from them. And you have worshipped the gods of silver and gold, of brass, iron, wood, and stone. But you have not glorified the God who holds your life in his hand."

Then Daniel said, "This is the writing that was written: MENE, MENE, TEKEL, UPHARSIN ("Numbered, Weighed, and Divided"). And this is what the writing means: God has numbered the days of your kingdom, and finished it. You are weighed on the balance scales, and are found lacking. Your kingdom is divided and is given to the Medes and Persians." That very night, King Belshazzar was killed; and then Darius the Mede took over the kingdom.

DANIEL 5

# DANIEL IN THE LION'S DEN

King Darius the Mede appointed one hundred and twenty princes to rule over the whole kingdom. He preferred Daniel above the others, and set him over them all. These men tried to find fault with Daniel, but they could find none. They said, "We shall not find any chance to complain against Daniel, except where it concerns the law of his God."

Then they went to King Darius and said, "We have decided to issue an order that anyone who asks a favor of any god or man for thirty days shall be put in the den of lions." And King Darius signed the order.

Even though Daniel knew that the king had signed the order, he knelt three times a day, and prayed. Then he gave thanks to his God, as he had done before.

The men found him praying, and they went to King Darius, and they said, "Daniel does not pay attention to you, O king, or to your order. He kneels three times a day to pray to his God."

When the king heard this, he was not pleased, and he set his heart on saving Daniel. But the men said, "You know it is our law: no order that the king gives may be changed."

So the king ordered that Daniel be put into the den of lions. But then he said to him, "Your God whom you serve always, he will deliver you." And a stone was put over the mouth of the den.

Then the king went to his palace, but he could not eat or sleep. Early in the morning he arose and hurried to the den of lions. When he came to the den he cried out in a sad voice, "O Daniel, has your God been able to save you from the lions?"

And Daniel said to the king, "My God has sent his angel and has shut the lions' mouths, and they have not hurt me. For I have been found innocent before God, and before you."

The king was very glad for Daniel, and he had him taken from the den of lions. And there was not a mark or a hurt upon Daniel, because he believed in his God.

King Darius put the men who had accused Daniel into the den of lions, and the lions overpowered them.

Then the king wrote to his people, saying, "Let all fear the God of Daniel, the living God whose kingdom will not be destroyed. For God works many signs and wonders in heaven and on earth, and God has saved Daniel from the power of the lions."

DANIEL 6

# JONAH AND THE WHALE

The word of the Lord came to Jonah, the son of Amittai, saying, "Arise now, and go up to Nineveh, that great city, and warn the people there that I will destroy them because of their wickedness." But Jonah fled from the presence of the Lord, and he boarded a ship for Tarshish.

But the Lord sent out a great wind, and there was a mighty storm in the sea, so strong that it seemed as if the ship would break apart. The sailors were afraid, and each man cried to his god. And they threw the cargo into the sea to lighten the ship.

The sailors said to one another, "Let us cast lots to see who has brought this evil upon us." So they cast lots, and the lot fell on Jonah.

They said to him, "Of what people are you? And what have you done to bring this evil upon us?" And Jonah answered them, "I am a Hebrew; and I fear the Lord, the God of heaven, who has made the sea and the dry land."

Then Jonah told them that he had fled from the presence of the Lord. They were very frightened, and said, "What shall we do to you, so that the sea will be calm for us?" And Jonah said, "Throw me into the sea, and it will grow calm, for I know it is because of me that this great storm has come upon you." But the men rowed hard to bring the ship to land. But the sea was too rough, and they could not reach it.

So they took up Jonah, and they threw him into the sea. And the sea stopped raging. Then the men greatly feared the Lord, and they offered a sacrifice and made vows to him. Then the Lord prepared a great fish to swallow Jonah. And Jonah was in the belly of the fish for three days and three nights.

Then Jonah prayed to the Lord from out of the fish's belly, and said, "O Lord my God, I am sent out of your sight, yet I will look again toward your holy temple. And I will sacrifice to you with the voice of thanksgiving." And the Lord spoke to the fish, and it spit up Jonah out upon the dry land.

Then the word of the Lord came to Jonah the second time, saying, "Arise, and go up to Nineveh, that great city, and preach as I have told you." So Jonah went to Nineveh, as the Lord commanded.

And as Jonah entered the city, he began crying out, "In forty days, Nineveh shall be destroyed." And the people of Nineveh believed God, and proclaimed a fast. From the greatest of them to the least of them, they repented of their evil. When God saw that they had turned from their evil way, he repented, and he did not destroy them.

But this displeased Jonah, and he was very angry. And he said to the Lord, "Did I not flee from you, because I knew that you are a gracious God, and merciful, and slow to anger, and one who repents of evil? Now, I beg you, take my life, for it is better for me to die than to live." Then the Lord said, "Are you right to be so angry?"

So Jonah went out, and he made himself a shelter on the east side of the city. He sat under it, so that he might see what would become of the city.

And the Lord God made a vine grow over the shelter to shade Jonah's head. And Jonah was very glad of the vine.

But in the morning, God sent a worm to eat away at the vine until it dried up and died. And when the sun rose, God sent a hot east wind. And the sun beat upon Jonah's unshaded head until he grew faint, and wished again to die.

Then God said to Jonah, "Are you right to be angry at the vine?"

Jonah said, "I am right to be angry, angry enough to die."

And then the Lord said, "You have pity for this vine, which you did neither plant nor take care of, and which came up in a night, and then died in a night.

"Should I not then pity Nineveh, that great city, in which there are more than one hundred twenty thousand persons who cannot tell their right hand from their left, and also many cattle?"

JONAH 1–4

# The
# *New Testament*

# THE COMING OF THE WORD

*I*n the beginning was the Word, and the Word was with God, and the Word was God.

He was in the beginning with God. All things were made by him, and without him nothing was made.

In him was life, and the life was the light of men. For the true light shines in the darkness, and the darkness cannot overcome it.

And the Word was made flesh, and lived among us. We have seen his glory, the glory of the only true son of the Father, full of grace and truth.

JOHN 1:1–5, 14

# ZACHARIAS AND ELIZABETH

There was in the days of Herod, the king of Judea, a certain priest named Zacharias. His wife was of the family of Aaron, and her name was Elizabeth. They were both righteous before God, following all the laws and commandments of the Lord.

But they had no child, because Elizabeth could not give birth. And both of them were old, far along in years.

And so it came to pass, while Zacharias carried out his priest's duties in the temple, an angel of the Lord appeared to him, standing on the right side of the altar. And when Zacharias saw the angel, he was troubled, and fear fell upon him.

But the angel said to him, "Fear not, Zacharias. Your prayer has been heard. Your wife Elizabeth shall give you a son, and you shall call him by the name John. And you will have joy and happiness, and many will give thanks at his birth. He shall be great in the sight of the Lord, and shall be filled with the Holy Spirit, even within his mother's body."

And Zacharias said to the angel, "How shall I know this? For I am an old man, and my wife is far along in years."

And the angel answered him, "I am Gabriel who stands in the presence of God, and I am sent to speak to you, to show you this good news. And behold, you will be without voice, and not able to speak, until the day when these things shall be performed. This is so because you did not believe my words, which will come true in their time."

The people were waiting for Zacharias outside the sanctuary. They wondered why he had delayed so long there. And when he came out, he could not speak, and they realized that he had seen a vision.

And it came to pass that, as soon as his work at the temple was done, Zacharias went to his own house. And after those days his wife Elizabeth was to have a child.

Luke 1:5–24

154

# THE ANGEL COMES TO MARY

And in the sixth month the angel Gabriel was sent from God to a city of Galilee, named Nazareth. He was sent to a young woman in this city, a virgin girl named Mary. She was promised in marriage to a man whose name was Joseph, of the house of King David.

And the angel came to Mary and said, "Hail, you are highly favored. The Lord is with you. Blessed are you among women."

And when Mary saw him, she was troubled at what he said, and she wondered what kind of greeting this might be.

And the angel said to her, "Fear not, Mary, for you have found favor with God. And you will be with child, and you will give birth to a son, and you will call his name JESUS."

Then Mary said to the angel, "How will this come to be, when I have never been with a man?"

The angel answered and said to her, "The Holy Spirit will come upon you, and the power of the Highest will overshadow you. And the holy being that will be born of you will be called the Son of God."

LUKE 1:26–35

# THE SHEPHERDS COME

And there were in this same country shepherds staying in the fields, keeping watch over their flock by night.

And suddenly the angel of the Lord came upon them, and the glory of the Lord shone around them, and they were very afraid.

The angel said to them, "Fear not, for behold, I bring you good news, news of great joy, which shall be for all people. For to you is born this day in the city of David a Savior, who is Christ the Lord.

"And this shall be a sign to you: You shall find the baby wrapped in swaddling clothes, lying in a manger."

And suddenly there was with the angel a multitude of the heavenly band of angels, praising God and saying, "Glory to God in the highest, and on earth peace, good will toward men."

And then it came to pass, after the angels had gone away from them into heaven, that the shepherds said to one another, "Let us go now, to Bethlehem, and see this thing that has happened, that the Lord has made known to us."

And so they came with haste, and they found Mary and Joseph, and the babe lying in a manger.

And when they had seen this, they went out and made known to all those they met, the things that were told to them by the angel about this child.

And all the people who heard the good news were amazed at the things the shepherds told them.

LUKE 2:8–17

# THE WISE MEN VISIT JESUS

Now when Jesus was born in Bethlehem, behold, there came wise men from the East to Jerusalem. They said, "Where is he that is born the King of the Jews? We have seen his star in the East, and we have come to worship him."

When Herod the king heard these things, he was troubled, and he gathered all the chief priests and scribes of the people together. He demanded that they tell him where this Christ could have been born.

And they said to him, "In Bethlehem of Judea, for so it is written by the prophet. It is said, 'You, Bethlehem, out of you shall come a leader, and he shall rule my people, Israel.'"

Then King Herod called the wise men to speak with him in secret, and he asked the men to tell him exactly at what time the star had appeared.

And he sent them to Bethlehem, and said, "Go, and search carefully for the young child. And when you have found him, return and bring me word of him, so that I may go and worship him also."

When the wise men had heard the king, they departed. And then they saw the same star that they had seen in the East, and it went before them, until it came and stopped over the place where the young child was.

And when the wise men saw this star, they were filled with great joy.

They came to the house, and they saw the young child with his mother Mary. The wise men fell to the ground, and they worshipped him. And then they opened their treasures, and they presented the gifts they had brought for him: gold, and frankincense, and myrrh.

But then the wise men were warned by God in a dream not to return to Herod. And so they went back to their own country, but by a different way.

MATTHEW 2:1–12

# THE BOY IN THE TEMPLE

Now, Jesus's parents went up from Nazareth to Jerusalem every year at the feast of the Passover. And when Jesus was twelve years old, they went to Jerusalem, as was the custom of the feast. And when the feast was ended, they returned home. But the child Jesus stayed behind in Jerusalem. And Joseph and Mary did not know this.

His parents, thinking him to be in their group of travelers, had already made a day's journey away from the city. And so they searched for Jesus among their relatives and friends. But they did not find him. And when they did not find him, they turned back to Jerusalem, and they searched for him there. But still they did not find him.

Then, after three days, they found Jesus. He was in the temple, sitting among the teachers, both listening to them and asking them questions. And all who heard him were astonished at his understanding and his answers.

When his parents saw him, they were amazed, and his mother said "Son, why have you treated us so? See how we have suffered as we searched for you."

Jesus said, "Why did you search for me? Didn't you know I must be about my Father's business?" But they did not understand what he had said to them.

Then Jesus went down with them to Nazareth, and he obeyed them. But his mother kept all these sayings in her heart. And Jesus grew in wisdom and in stature, and in favor with God and man.

LUKE 2:40–51

167

# JOHN BAPTIZES JESUS

*I*t was written by the prophet: "I will send my messenger, and he shall prepare the way before you."

Then in those days came John, the son of Zacharias, preaching in the wilderness of Judea, and saying, "Repent, for the kingdom of heaven is at hand. For this is what was spoken by the prophet Isaiah, who said, 'The voice of one crying in the wilderness. Prepare the way of the Lord: Make his paths straight. Every valley shall be filled, and every mountain and hill shall be brought low; and the crooked shall be made straight, and the rough places shall be made smooth. And all who are living shall see the salvation of God.'"

Now John wore a coat of camel's hair, and a leather belt around his waist. His food was locusts and wild honey.

Then all the people of the land of Judea went out to John, and all the people of Jerusalem. And John baptized them in the Jordan River, as they confessed their sins. And so the people thought of John in their hearts, and they wondered if he were the Christ.

John answered the people, saying to them, "One who is much greater than I is coming. I am not even worthy to stoop down and untie his sandals. I indeed have baptized you with water, but he will baptize you with the Holy Spirit, and with fire."

It came to pass in those days, that Jesus came from Nazareth of Galilee, where John was baptizing the people. John saw Jesus coming and he said, "Behold, here is the Lamb of God, who takes away the sins of the world!"

Now Jesus had come to be baptized by John in the Jordan River. But at first John refused him, saying, "Why do you come to me? I need to be baptized by you instead."

Then Jesus answered, saying to him, "Let it be so for now; for we should fulfill all righteousness." So John agreed to baptize Jesus.

And Jesus, when he was baptized, came up immediately from the water. And the heavens were opened to him, and he saw the Spirit of God descending like a dove, and coming down upon him.

And a voice came from heaven, saying, "You are my beloved Son; with you I am well pleased."

MATTHEW 3; MARK 1; LUKE 3; JOHN 1

# JESUS IS TEMPTED

*J*esus returned from the Jordan River full of the Holy Spirit. And then he was led by the Spirit into the wilderness, and there he was tempted by the devil.

Jesus was there in the wilderness with the wild beasts, and he went without food for forty days and forty nights. And when those forty days and forty nights had ended, Jesus was very hungry.

Then the devil came to Jesus, and he said, "If you are the Son of God, command that these stones be made into bread."

But Jesus answered, "It has been written, 'Man does not live by bread alone, but by every word that comes from the mouth of God.'"

And then the devil took Jesus up into the holy city of Jerusalem, and set him on the highest place in the holy temple. And the devil said to Jesus, "If you are the Son of God, throw yourself down from here; for it is written, 'He shall have his angels watch over you and guard you; in their hands they will carry you up, so that you will not strike your foot against a stone.'"

But Jesus said to him, "It is also written, 'You shall not tempt the Lord your God.'"

Then the devil took Jesus to the top of a very high mountain. In one moment of time, he showed Jesus all the kingdoms of the world, and all the glory of them. And the devil said to Jesus, "All this power I will give you, and all the glory of them. It will all be yours, if only you will fall down and worship me."

But Jesus said to him, "Get away from me, Satan! For it is written, 'You shall worship the Lord your God, and only him shall you serve.'" Then the devil left Jesus, and the angels came and cared for him.

And so then Jesus returned in the power of the Holy Spirit to Galilee, and a report of him went out to all the surrounding country.

MATTHEW 4; MARK 1; LUKE 4

# JESUS AND HIS DISCIPLES

Then Jesus came to live in the city of Capernaum, which is on the shore of the lake known as the Sea of Galilee. And Jesus was about thirty years of age when he set out on his ministry.

From that time on, Jesus began to preach, saying, "The hour has now come, and the kingdom of God is near at hand. Turn away from all the wrongs that you have done, and believe in the Gospel, the good news of the Lord."

Now one day as Jesus walked by the Sea of Galilee, he saw two brothers: Simon, who is also called Peter, and his brother Andrew. They were casting a net into the sea, for they were fishermen. And Jesus said to them, "Follow me, and I will make you fishers of men."

And immediately they left their nets, and they followed Jesus.

And then when Jesus had gone a little while farther, he saw two more brothers, James the son of Zebedee, and John his brother. They were in a boat with Zebedee their father, mending their nets; and Jesus called to them. And they immediately left their father in the boat with the hired servants, and they followed after Jesus.

And Jesus went all over Galilee, teaching in the synagogues, and preaching the Gospel, the good news of the kingdom of heaven, and healing all kinds of sickness among the people.

And so the name of Jesus spread throughout all Syria. Sick people who suffered from all kinds of diseases and pains were brought to him, and Jesus healed them all. Great crowds of people followed after Jesus; people from Galilee, and from Decapolis, and from the city of Jerusalem, and from Judea, and from beyond the Jordan River.

And one day as Jesus passed through the city of Capernaum, he saw a man named Matthew, a tax collector, sitting in his tax office. And Jesus said to Matthew, "Follow me." And then Matthew arose, and followed him.

Then Jesus sat down to eat with Matthew, and many tax collectors and sinners came and sat down with Jesus and his disciples. And when the Pharisees saw this, they asked the disciples, "Why does your master eat with tax collectors, and with sinners?"

But Jesus heard their question, and he answered, "It is not those who are healthy who need a doctor; it is those who are sick. Go and learn what this means. 'I want mercy, and not sacrifice. For I am here not to call those who already do right, but to call those who do evil, to change their ways.'"

Now, these are the names of the twelve Apostles: the first, Simon, whom Jesus called Peter, and his brother, Andrew; James the son of Zebedee, and his brother John; Philip, and Bartholomew, and Thomas; Matthew the tax collector; James the son of Alphaeus, and Thaddaeus, and Simon the Canaanite; and Judas Iscariot, who later betrayed Jesus.

MATTHEW 4, 9, 10; MARK 1–3; LUKE 3, 6; JOHN 1

173

# JESUS ANGERS THE PEOPLE

*J*esus came to Nazareth, where he had been brought up. As was his custom, he went into the synagogue on the sabbath day, and stood up to read.

The book of the prophet Isaiah was given to him. Jesus opened the book and found the place where it was written, "The Spirit of the Lord is upon me; he has chosen me to preach the good news to the poor. He has sent me to heal the brokenhearted, to set free the captives, to give sight to the blind, and to bring comfort to all those who suffer."

Then Jesus closed the book, and he gave it back. He sat down, and the eyes of all who were in the synagogue were fixed on him. And he began to say, "This day the scripture has come true in your hearing."

But the people asked themselves, "Who is this man? Is he not the son of Joseph?"

Jesus heard this and said to them, "You will surely tell to me the old saying, 'Physician, heal yourself! We have heard of the things you did in Capernaum. Do them here also, in your own country.'"

And then Jesus said to them, "Truly I say to you, no prophet is accepted in his own country. There were many widows in Israel in the days of Elijah the prophet, when the heavens were shut up for three years and six months, and no rains came. There was a great famine throughout all the land. But Elijah was not sent to save any of them, but only to the land of Sidon, to a woman who was a widow there. And there were many who were sick in Israel in the time of Elijah, and none of them were healed, but only Naaman, a Syrian."

When the people in the synagogue heard this, they were filled with anger. They rose up, and they forced Jesus out of the city. They led him to the top of a hill, where they could throw him down headfirst. But Jesus passed through the midst of them and went on his way.

LUKE 4:16–30

# JESUS AND NATHANAEL

One day Jesus decided to go to Galilee. He found Philip and said to him, "Follow me." Philip was from the town of Bethesda, the city of Andrew and Peter.

Philip found Nathanael, and said to him, "We have found him. We have found the one that Moses spoke of in the law, and the one that the prophets wrote about. He is Jesus of Nazareth, the son of Joseph."

But Nathanael said to Philip, "Nazareth? Can anything good come out of Nazareth?"

So Philip said to him, "Come and see."

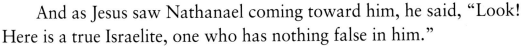

And as Jesus saw Nathanael coming toward him, he said, "Look! Here is a true Israelite, one who has nothing false in him."

And Nathanael said to Jesus, "But how did you know me?"

Jesus answered and said to him, "Before Philip called to you, I saw you sitting under the fig tree."

And so Nathanael answered and said to Jesus, "Rabbi, Teacher, you are truly the Son of God; you are truly the King of Israel."

But Jesus answered him, "Just because I said, 'I saw you under the fig tree,' you will believe in me? You will see much greater things than that. Truly, truly, I say to you, now you will see heaven open, and the angels of God rise up and come down upon the Son of man."

JOHN 1:43–51

# THE WEDDING FEAST AT CANA

Once there was a wedding in the town of Cana, in Galilee. Mary the mother of Jesus was there. And both Jesus and his disciples were invited to the wedding feast. The wedding guests wanted more wine, and Mary said to Jesus, "They have no wine." Then she spoke to the servants and said, "Whatever he tells you to do, you do it." Standing nearby there were six large water pots made of stone.

Jesus said to the servants, "Fill these pots with water." They filled them up to the brim. Then he said, "Take some out now, and bring it to the master of the feast." And so they did this.

The water had been made into wine. When the master of the feast tasted this wine, he did not know where it had come from. But the servants knew. Then the master called to the bridegroom, and he said to him, "Other men serve their good wine at the beginning, and then, when their guests have finished this, bring out the poorer wine. But you have saved the best wine for last."

And so water was turned into wine at Cana in Galilee. This was the beginning of the miracles of Jesus.

JOHN 2:1–11

# A MAN MUST BE BORN AGAIN

There was in Jerusalem at that time a man of the Pharisees, who was called Nicodemus, a ruler of the Jews. This man came to Jesus by night, and he said to him, "We know you are a teacher who has come from God. No man could do the miracles that you do, unless God is with him."

Jesus answered him, "Truly, truly, I say to you, unless a man is born again, he cannot see the kingdom of heaven."

Nicodemus said to him, "How can a man be born when he is old? Can he enter a second time into his mother's body, and be born?"

And then Jesus answered him, "Unless a man is born of water and the Holy Spirit, he cannot enter the kingdom of God. Do not wonder that I have said to you, 'You must be born again.' The wind blows where it wishes, and you hear the sound of the wind. But you do not know where the wind comes from or where it goes. So it is with those who are born of the Spirit."

Nicodemus answered and said, "But how can these things be?"

Jesus said, "If I have told you things of earth, and you do not believe, how can you believe when I tell you things of heaven? For no man has gone up into heaven, but he who came down from heaven."

And then Jesus said, "For God so loved the world that he gave his only begotten Son, that whosoever believes in him shall not perish, but will have everlasting life."

JOHN 3:1–16

177

# THE LIVING WATER

Jesus came to a city of Samaria, called Sychar. This city was near to the piece of land that Jacob gave to his son Joseph. Now, Jacob's own well was there, and Jesus, being tired from his journey, sat down at the well. His disciples had gone away into the city to buy food.

A woman of Samaria came to the well to get water. Jesus said to her, "Give me a drink."

The Samaritan woman said to him, "How is it that you, a Jew, can ask me, a woman of Samaria, to give you a drink?" For the Jews have nothing to do with the people of Samaria.

Jesus answered and said to her, "If you knew the gift of God, and if you knew who has said to you, 'Give me a drink,' then you would have asked him, and he would have given you living water."

The woman said to Jesus, "Sir, you have nothing to take up the water with, and the well is very deep. From where do you get this living water? Are you greater than our father Jacob, who gave us this well, and who drank from it himself?"

Jesus said, "Whoever drinks this water will soon be thirsty again. But whoever drinks of the water that I give him, will never be thirsty. For the water I give will become a spring of water that flows inside him, springing up to give everlasting life."

JOHN 4:1–14

# A DYING CHILD LIVES

Jesus came into Cana of Galilee, the place where he had made the water into wine. There was in the city a certain high officer of the king. The son of this officer was sick in Capernaum. When this man heard that Jesus had come out of Judea into Galilee, he went to Jesus. And he begged Jesus to come and heal his son, who was at the point of death.

And Jesus said to the officer, "Unless you see signs and wonders, you will not believe." The officer said to him, "Sir, come down before my child dies."

Jesus said to him, "Go on your way now. Your son will live." The man believed the words that Jesus had spoken to him, and he went on his way. And as he was going down to his home, his servants met him, and they said to him, "Your son lives."

Then the man asked the servants to tell him the time when his son had begun to get better. And they said, "It was yesterday, at the seventh hour. It was then that the fever left him."

The father knew it had been at this same hour that Jesus had said, "Your son will live." And so this man believed in Jesus. This was the second miracle of Jesus, after he had come out of Judea into Galilee.

JOHN 4:46–54

# JESUS CALLS TO SIMON

Then it came to pass one day, as Jesus stood by the Sea of Galilee, that the people pressed in all around him, wanting to hear the word of God.

Then Jesus saw two boats that were standing by the shore, but the fishermen had gone out of them, and they were washing their nets. So Jesus got into one of the boats. This was the boat of Simon, who is also called Peter.

Jesus asked Simon to take him out a little way from the shore. And then Jesus sat down in the boat, and he taught the people from the boat. And when Jesus had finished speaking to the people, he said to Simon, "Take your boat out into the deep water, and let down your nets there for a catch."

But Simon answered him, "Master, we have fished all night, and we have caught nothing! Still, I will follow your word and let down the nets."

When Simon had done this, the nets closed in on a great number of fish, so many that the nets were breaking. And Simon called out to his partners, the fishermen in the other boat, to come and help him.

And so these fishermen came, but there were so many fish that they filled both boats, and the boats began to sink.

When Simon Peter saw this, he fell down at Jesus's knees, and he cried, "Go away from me, for I am a sinful man, O Lord." For he was amazed, as were all those who were with him, at the catch of fish that they had taken.

And James and John, the sons of Zebedee, were amazed also; they were the partners of Simon. But then Jesus said to Simon, "Do not be afraid. From now on you will catch men instead of fish."

LUKE 5:1–10

# JESUS HEALS THE SICK

Jesus and his disciples were in Capernaum. On the sabbath day, Jesus entered the synagogue and taught. And the people were astonished at his teaching, for he taught them as one who had authority, and not as the scribes did.

In the synagogue there was a man who had within him a demon, an unclean spirit, who cried out, "What have you to do with us, you Jesus of Nazareth? Have you come to destroy us? I know who you are, the Holy One of God."

Jesus said to the unclean spirit, "Be silent! Come out of this man!" And the unclean spirit caused the man's body to twist and his voice to cry out loudly. Then the spirit came out of him.

The people were all amazed, and they asked among themselves, "What thing is this? What new teaching is this? This Jesus has the power to command even the unclean spirits, and to make them obey him."

And so the name of Jesus became known everywhere, throughout all the regions around Galilee.

Then Jesus came out of the synagogue and entered the house of Simon and Andrew, with James and John. Now the mother of Simon's wife was sick with a fever, and they told Jesus of this.

Jesus came and took her by the hand, and he lifted her up. The fever left her immediately, and she got up to serve them.

In the evening, when the sun went down, they brought to Jesus all those who were sick with many different diseases. Jesus laid his hands on every one of them, and he healed them. And all the city was gathered together outside his door.

And once there came to Jesus a man who was sick with leprosy, a terrible disease of the skin. And the man fell to his knees before Jesus, crying out, "If you will, you can heal me, and make me clean again."

And Jesus, moved with pity for this man, reached out his hand and said to him, "I will; be clean." And as soon as Jesus had spoken, the leprosy went out from the man, and left him, and he was clean again.

And as Jesus sent the man away, he told him, "Say nothing to anyone, but go on your way. Show yourself to the priest, and do this in return for being made clean: offer the gift that Moses commanded, as proof to the people that you are healed."

But the man went out, and he began to tell everyone of his healing, and to spread the news everywhere. So many people knew of it that Jesus could no longer freely enter the city. His fame went ahead of him, and many great crowds came together to hear him, and to be cured of their illnesses.

And so Jesus left the city, and he went away to the wilderness by himself, and there he prayed.

MARK 1:21–45; LUKE 4:31–42; 5:12–16

183

# A SICK MAN WALKS AGAIN

Some days after this, Jesus came back again to Capernaum. Everyone was told that Jesus was in someone's house. And so many people came right away to gather together there. But so many people came that there was no room for them to get in, or even to stand at the door. And Jesus was preaching the word to them.

Then some people came to see Jesus, bringing a man who was paralyzed and could not move. He lay on a bed, and he was carried by four men. They tried to carry this paralyzed man into the house, to bring him close to Jesus. But they could not find a way to bring him in, because of the great crowd around the house.

And so they went up upon the housetop, carrying the man on his bed. They broke open a hole in the roof. When the roof was opened up, they lowered the bed down through the hole, with the sick man on it, into the room where Jesus was.

And when Jesus saw the sick man at his feet, and when he saw their faith, he said to the man, "My son, your sins are forgiven."

But there were certain of the scribes and the Pharisees sitting there, and they began to ask themselves, "Why does this man speak in such a wrong way? Only God can forgive sins."

But when Jesus sensed their thoughts, he answered and said to them, "What are you thinking in your hearts? Is it easier to say to this man, 'Your sins are forgiven' or to say to him 'Rise up, take up your bed, and walk?' I say this so that you will know that the Son of man has the power on earth to forgive sins."

And then Jesus turned to the sick man and he said, "I say to you: Rise, and take up your bed, and go on your way to your own house."

Immediately the man rose up before them, and he took up the bed, and he went out through the crowd. All who saw it were amazed, and they praised God, saying, "Never have we seen such a thing as this!"

MARK 2:1–12; LUKE 5:17–26

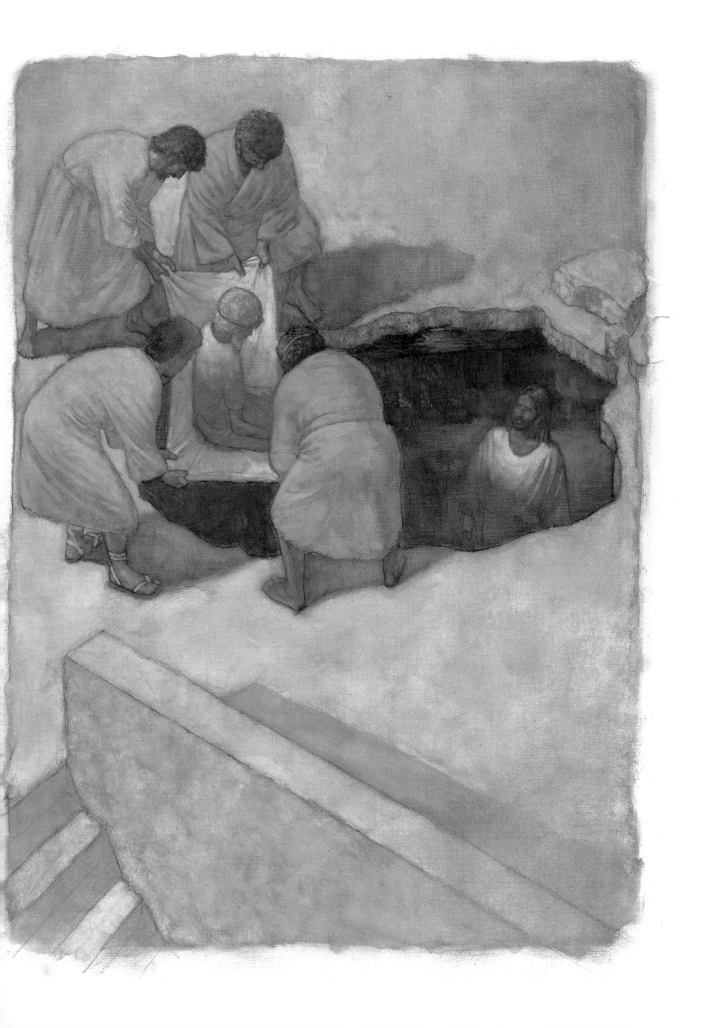

# THE SERMON ON THE MOUNT

Seeing the great crowds that followed him, Jesus went up on a hill. And when he had sat down, his disciples came to him. And Jesus began to teach them, saying these words:

*"Blessed are the poor in spirit, for theirs is the kingdom of heaven.*

*"Blessed are those who mourn, for they shall be comforted.*

*"Blessed are the meek, for they shall inherit the earth.*

*"Blessed are those who hunger and thirst for what is right, for they shall be satisfied.*

*"Blessed are the merciful, for they shall receive mercy.*

*"Blessed are the pure in heart, for they shall see God.*

*"Blessed are the peacemakers, for they shall be called the children of God.*

*"Blessed are those who are persecuted for the sake of righteousness, for theirs is the kingdom of heaven.*

*"Blessed are you when men insult you, and persecute you, and speak all kinds of evil against you falsely, on my account. Give thanks and be very glad, for your reward will be great in heaven. For in this same way, men persecuted the prophets who came before you."*

And then Jesus raised his eyes to look at his disciples, and he said, "You are the salt of the earth. But if the salt has lost its flavor, how shall its saltiness be restored? It is then no good for anything but to be thrown out on the ground and walked upon.

"You are the light of the world. A city that is set on a hill cannot be hidden. People do not light a lamp and put it under a bushel; they put it on a stand. Then it gives light to all who are in the house. So let your light shine out before all, so that they may see your good works, and give glory to your Father who is in heaven."

186

, "Do not think that I come to destroy the law
ets. I am not here to destroy the law, but to see
truly, I say to you, until heaven and earth pass
letter, not one dot, will pass from the law, until all

reaks one of the commandments, or who teaches
s, shall be called least in the kingdom of heaven. But
who ws God's commandments, and teaches others to do the
same, shall be called great in the kingdom of heaven. For I say to you:
It is not enough to only do right. Unless you are more righteous than
the scribes and the Pharisees, you shall not enter the kingdom of
heaven."

Then Jesus said, "You have heard that it was said in the days of
old, 'You shall not kill, and whoever kills will be subject to judgment.'
But I say to you: Whoever is angry with his brother without cause, or
who insults his brother, shall be in danger of the judgment. So if you
bring a gift to the altar, and you remember there that your brother has
something against you, put your gift down. First go and find your
brother and make peace with him, and then come and offer your gift.

"You have heard that it was said, 'An eye for an eye, and a tooth
for a tooth.' But I say to you: Do not resist one who is evil. Whoever
strikes you on the right cheek, turn the other cheek to him also. And if
someone should sue you to take your shirt, give to him your coat also.
And if you are forced to go a mile with someone, go with him for two
miles. And give to anyone who begs from you, and do not turn away
anyone who would borrow from you.

"You have heard that it was said, 'You shall love your neighbor,
and hate your enemy.' But I say to you: Love even your enemies. Bless
those who curse you. Do good to those who hate you, and pray for
those who persecute you. Then you will be the children of your Father
in heaven, for he makes the sun shine both on the evil and on the good,
and sends rain both to those who do right and those who do wrong."

MATTHEW 5; LUKE 6

# JESUS SAVES A CHILD

Once while Jesus was speaking, a certain leader of the synagogue came to him. This man's name was Jairus. He fell to the ground at the feet of Jesus, and he begged Jesus to come to his house.

Jairus said, "My little daughter lies at the point of death. I pray to you, come and put your hand on her, so that she may be healed, and live." For Jairus had only one daughter, about twelve years of age, and she lay dying.

So Jesus got up, and he followed after the man, and so did all of the crowd with him. But then some people came from the house of Jairus, and they said to him, "Your daughter is already dead. Why do you trouble the Master any further?"

But Jesus ignored the others and he said to Jairus, "Do not fear, only believe, and your daughter will be made well." Then he allowed no one to come with him, except Peter and James and John the brother of James.

And when they came to the house of Jairus, Jesus saw a crowd of people in great confusion, and he heard them all crying and shouting loudly. And when Jesus had entered the house, he said to them, "Why do you make such a noise, and weep? This child is not dead, she is only sleeping." And then they laughed at him, knowing that she was dead.

But Jesus put them all to one side, and he took the child's father and mother and his disciples and he went in where the child was lying. And he took the child by the hand, and he said to her, "Little girl, I say to you: Get up."

And immediately the little girl got up, and she walked. And Jesus ordered them to give her something to eat.

All the people who were there were amazed at what they had seen. And so the fame of Jesus was spread throughout all the land.

MATTHEW 9; MARK 5; LUKE 8

# JESUS SPEAKS IN PARABLES

*J*esus often said things to the people in parables, stories that he told to teach a lesson. Once he told them this parable.

"One day a farmer went out to sow his seeds. And when he threw his seeds down upon the ground, some of them fell by the wayside, and the birds came and ate them up. And some fell in rocky places, where there was little dirt. So these seeds came up right away, because the soil was not very deep. But when the sun rose, those seeds were scorched. They had no roots, and so they withered away.

"And then there were other seeds that fell among weeds and thorns, and the weeds sprang up, and choked them. But there were some seeds that fell on good ground, and they grew well and brought forth good grain. Now, he who has ears, let him hear this."

And later when Jesus was alone with his disciples, they asked him, "What might this parable mean?"

Jesus said, "You have been given the power to know the secrets of the kingdom of God. But for other people, all these things are only parables. These people look, but they do not really see. And they listen, but they do not really hear. Now, here is what this parable means.

"The seed that the farmer sows is the word of God. And there are some people who hear this, but who still stay by the wayside. And the devil comes to them and takes away the word that was sown in their hearts.

"And there are others who are like the seeds that were sown on rocky ground. When they hear the word, they receive it with joy. But these people have no root in themselves, and so they believe only for a while, and then in time of temptation they fall away.

"And the seeds that were choked among the weeds are like those people who, when they have heard the word, are choked with cares and riches and pleasures of this life.

"And then there are those who are like the seeds in the good soil, the ones with an honest and good heart. They have heard the word, and they keep it, and they bring forth good fruit."

And then he put another parable to them, saying, "The kingdom of heaven is like a grain of mustard seed, which a man took and sowed in his field. The mustard seed is indeed the smallest of all the seeds sown on earth. But when it is sown, it grows up and becomes the greatest of all herbs. It puts out large branches, and it becomes a tree, so that the birds of the air can come and make nests in the branches.

"And the kingdom of heaven is like treasure that is hidden in a field, which a man has found and covered up. And so he goes and sells all that he has and buys this field.

"And the kingdom of heaven is like a merchant, who is searching for precious pearls. And when he has found one pearl of great value, he goes and sells all that he has to buy it.

"The kingdom of heaven is also like a net that is thrown into the sea to catch fish of every kind. When the net is full, the men draw it into shore, and they sit down. They gather the good fish in baskets, but they throw the bad fish away. So it will be at the end of the world, when the angels come to separate the wicked people from the good."

And so Jesus spoke to the people in this way, with many parables. And nothing that he said to them was without a parable.

MATTHEW 13; MARK 4; LUKE 8

# THE LOAVES AND THE FISHES

Jesus went out, and he saw a great crowd. He was moved with feeling for them, because they were like sheep without a shepherd. And he began to teach the people many things, and he healed those who were sick.

When the day was coming to an end, and evening was near, the disciples came to Jesus, saying to him, "This is a lonely place, and the hour is now late. Send the crowd away, so that they may go into the towns and country near here, and buy themselves food, for they have nothing to eat."

But Jesus said to them, "They do not have to leave. You give them something to eat."

But the disciples said to him, "We have no food here. There is a small boy who has five loaves of barley bread, and two fishes. But what good is that when there are so many here?"

200

And Jesus said, "Bring them here to me." And then Jesus ordered the crowd to sit down on the grass, and he took the five loaves and the two fishes. He looked up to heaven, and he blessed them, and he broke the bread, and he gave it to his disciples. The disciples gave it to the crowd. Jesus divided the two fish among them all.

And then all of the people did eat, and all were filled. Then Jesus said, "Gather up the bits that are left, so that nothing will be lost." And even then, the broken pieces of bread and the fish that were left over were enough to fill twelve baskets full.

There were about five thousand men who ate there that day, and women and children too. And when they had seen this miracle that Jesus did, they said, "This is surely the prophet who is to come into the world!"

MATTHEW 14; MARK 6; LUKE 9; JOHN 6

201

# JESUS SPEAKS OF FORGIVENESS

*J*esus said to his disciples, "If your brother does wrong to you, go straight to him and tell him his fault, between you and him alone. If he listens to you, then you have gained him as a brother to you again. But if he will not hear you, then take with you one or two more people as witnesses. With two or three witnesses, every word may then be confirmed by their evidence. And if he still refuses to listen to you, tell it to the church. And if he still refuses to listen even to the church, then treat him as you would one who does not believe in God. Treat him as you would treat a tax collector for the Romans.

"For truly I say to you, if two of you agree on earth about anything that you shall ask, it will be done for you by my father in heaven. For wherever two or three of you are gathered in my name, there I am in the midst of them."

Then Peter came up to Jesus and he said to him, "Lord, tell me, if my brother sins against me, how many times should I forgive him? Should I forgive him seven times?"

Jesus said to Peter, "No, I do not say to you, forgive him seven times. You must forgive him seventy-seven times.

"If your brother sins, correct him. And if he is truly sorry for what he has done and he stops doing it, then forgive him. Even if he does wrong to you seven times in one day, as long as he turns to you seven times and says, 'I repent. I am truly sorry and I will change my ways,' then you must forgive him."

Then Jesus told them this parable. He said, "The kingdom of heaven may be compared to a king who wished to settle his accounts with his servants. When he began to figure, one man was brought to the king who owed him ten thousand talents.

"Since the servant could not pay this debt, the king ordered him to be sold into slavery, and his wife, and his children too, so that the payment could be made.

"Then the servant fell down on his knees, and he begged the king, 'Have patience with me, and I will pay you all that I owe.'"

Now, a talent was a sum of money that it would take a worker several years to earn, so this man would have to work for hundreds of years to pay back what he owed.

Jesus said, "Therefore the king was moved with pity for the man, and he released him, and he forgave him the debt that he owed.

"Then this same servant went out and he met one of his fellow servants who owed him one hundred denarii. He put his hands on the other servant, and he grabbed him by the throat, and he said, 'Pay me what you owe!'"

Now, one denarius was a sum of money that it would take a worker less than one day to earn, so the other servant would have to work for only a few weeks to pay the man back what he owed.

Jesus said, "And so the other servant fell down on his knees, and he begged the man, 'Have patience with me, and I will pay you all that I owe.' But the man refused to do this, and he had his fellow servant thrown into prison, until he could pay his debt.

"And when the other servants saw what the man had done to his fellow servant, they were very sorry, and they went and told the king what had happened.

"So the king called the man back to him and he said, 'You evil servant! You begged me to forgive you, and so I forgave all that you owed. Should you not have mercy on your fellow servant, as I had mercy on you?' The king was very angry, and he sent the man to prison, to stay there until he had paid all of his debt.

"And so I say to you, my heavenly Father will do the same to every one of you, if you do not truly forgive your brother from your heart."

MATTHEW 18:15–35; LUKE 17:3–4

# THROWING THE FIRST STONE

Once the scribes and the Pharisees brought a woman to Jesus. She was guilty of adultery, the sin of having sex with a man who was not her husband.

They made this woman stand in the middle of their group, and they said to Jesus, "Teacher, this woman has been caught in the act of adultery. Now, the law of Moses has commanded us that persons who commit this sin shall be stoned to death. What do you say about her?"

By saying this, they hoped to trick Jesus into denying the law of Moses, so that they would have some charge to bring against him. Jesus bent down and wrote with his finger on the ground, as though he did not hear them.

# THE GOOD SAMARITAN

There was a certain man who had studied the law of Moses. This lawyer came to Jesus and asked him a question. He said to Jesus, "It is written in the law, 'Love your neighbor as you love yourself.' But who is my neighbor?" To answer him, Jesus said:

"A certain man of our land went down from Jerusalem to Jericho. On the way he was attacked by robbers. They stripped off his clothes, and beat him, and then went away, leaving him half dead.

"Now by chance a priest from our land was going down that same road. When the priest saw the hurt man, he passed by on the other side of the road.  And then a Levite came along, a man who worked for the priests in the temple. When the Levite saw the hurt man, he also passed by on the other side of the road.

"But then another man came along, a man from the foreign land of Samaria, someone our people think of as an enemy. And when this Samaritan saw the hurt man, he felt sorry for him. He went to him and tied up his wounds, pouring on oil and wine. Then the Samaritan put the man up on his own animal to ride. He brought him to an inn, and he took care of him.

"The next day before the Samaritan left, he took out two silver denarii. He gave these coins to the innkeeper, and he said, 'Take care of him with this money. If you spend more than this, then I will repay you when I come here again.'"

Then Jesus asked the lawyer, "Now, what do you think? Which one of those three who came along on the road was really the neighbor to the man who was robbed?"

And the lawyer answered, "It was the Samaritan. He was the one who showed mercy on the man."

And Jesus said, "You go out and do the same."

LUKE 10:29–37

215

# WORKERS IN THE VINEYARD

This is a story that Jesus told to his disciples about the kingdom of heaven. He said to them, "For the kingdom of heaven is like a man who owned a house and land. This man went out at six o'clock in the morning to hire some workers to work in his vineyard.

"The man agreed to pay these workers one silver coin each for the day's work. Then he sent them out into the vineyard.

"The man went out again at nine o'clock in the morning. He saw some other workers who were standing around in the marketplace, doing nothing. He said to them, 'You also go out into the vineyard, and I will pay you what is right for your work.' And so they went.

"And then the man went out again at twelve o'clock, and again at three o'clock in the afternoon. Both times he hired more workers in the same way. And then at five o'clock in the afternoon the man went out again, and he found others standing around doing nothing. He said to them, 'Why are you standing here idle all day long?'

"They said, 'Because no one has hired us to work.' The man said, 'You go into my vineyard. I will pay you what is right for your work.'

216

"And then when the end of the day had come, the man said to his chief servant, 'Call the workers now, and give them their pay. Begin with the last who was hired, and then go up to the first.'

"When the workers who had been hired at five o'clock in the afternoon came up, each of them received one silver coin. The workers who had been hired at six o'clock in the morning saw this, and when it was their turn to come up, they supposed that they would be paid more. But each of them also received one silver coin.

"When they got this, they were angry and complained to the man about their pay. They said to him, 'These last people worked for only one hour. You have made them equal to us, but we had to work all day under the hot sun.'

"The man answered and said to them, 'My friends, I did you no wrong. Did you not agree to work all day for me for one silver coin? That is a fair day's pay for this work. Take it then, and go on your way. Yes, I choose to give those who were hired last the same pay that I give to you. But is it not my right to do as I choose with what belongs to me? Are you jealous, because I am generous to these people?'

"And so the last shall be first, and the first shall be last. For many are called, but few are chosen."

MATTHEW 20:1–16

217

# THE STORY OF THE LOST SON

This parable also was told by Jesus. "Once there was a certain man who had two sons. The younger of the two sons went to his father and he said, 'Father, give me my share of the family property.' And so the father divided his property between his two sons.

"Not many days after this, the younger son gathered all his things together, and he made a journey into a far country. There he wasted all his money in wrong and foolish living.

"When he had spent all that he had, a great famine came upon the land, and the son was in great need. So then he had to go to work for a citizen of that country. That man sent the son out into the fields to feed the pigs. And the son was so hungry that he would gladly have eaten the scraps of food that the pigs were eating. But no one gave him anything.

"And then the son thought about this and said to himself, 'How many of my father's servants have enough food to eat, and even some to spare, while here I am dying of hunger! I will go to my father, and I will say to him, "Father, I have sinned against heaven, and against you. I am no longer worthy to be called your son. Take me as one of your servants."'

"And then the son got up, and he went to his father. But when he was still a long way off, his father saw him coming. He had great feeling for his son, and he ran to him, and held him, and kissed him.

"The son said to him, 'Father, I have sinned against heaven, and against you. I am no longer worthy to be called your son.'

"But the father said to his servants, 'Bring out the best robe, and put it on him. Put a ring on his hand, and shoes on his feet. And bring out the fatted calf and kill it for a feast, and let us eat, and be merry. For this is my son who was dead, and now he is alive again. He once was lost, and now he is found.' And so they began to celebrate.

"Now the older son was in the fields at this time, and as he came back and got closer to the house, he heard music and dancing. And he called to one of the servants and asked him what these things meant.

"And the servant said to him, 'Your brother has come back. Your father has killed the fatted calf for a feast, because your brother has come back to him safe and sound.'

"Then the older son was very angry, and he would not go into the house. His father came out to him, and he begged him to come in. The older son said to his father, 'All these many years I have served you, and I have never disobeyed your commands. Yet you never gave me even a small goat for a feast, so that I could celebrate with my friends. Now your other son has come home, the one who has wasted all your money, and you kill the fatted calf for him!'

"The father said to him, 'Son, you are here with me, and all that I have is yours. It was right that we should make merry, and be glad. For this is your brother who was dead, and now is alive. He was lost, and now is found.'"

LUKE 15:11–32

219

# A MAN RISES FROM THE DEAD

Martha was a woman from Bethany, a village close to the city of Jerusalem. She received Jesus as a guest in her house. Martha had a sister named Mary, who sat at the feet of Jesus and heard his words.

But Martha was bothered by all the work that she had to do in the house. She came to Jesus and said to him, "Lord, do you not care that my sister has left me to do the work alone? Please tell her to help me."

But Jesus answered her, "Martha, Martha, you are anxious and troubled about many different things. But there is only one thing that is really important, and Mary has chosen what is right. It should not be taken away from her."

Now, Mary and Martha also had a brother, named Lazarus. This man was very sick. His sisters sent word to Jesus, saying, "Lord, you must know this. The man that you dearly love is sick." For Jesus loved Martha, and her sister Mary, and Lazarus.

When Jesus heard that Lazarus was sick, he said, "This sickness is not unto death, but it is for the glory of God, so that the Son of God might be glorified by it."

Then Jesus stayed two more days in the same place where he was. After this, he said to his disciples, "Let us go into Judea again."

The disciples answered him, "Teacher, a little while ago the people who live there tried to kill you by stoning you. So why would you now go there again?"

And Jesus answered them, "Are there not twelve hours in the day? And if any man walks in the day, he does not stumble, because he sees the light of the world. But if he walks in the night, he will stumble, because there is no light in him."

Then Jesus said to them, "Come, our friend Lazarus sleeps. But I go to awaken him from this sleep."

The disciples said, "Lord, if he is sleeping, he will be well again."

His disciples thought that Jesus had said Lazarus was taking a rest by sleeping. But Jesus was speaking of the sleep of death.

And so Jesus then said plainly to them, "Lazarus is dead. For your sake, I am glad that I was not there. This was meant to be, so that now you may believe. Let us go to him."

Then one of the disciples spoke. This was Thomas, who was also called Didymus, the Twin. He said to the others, "Let us go also, so that we may die with him." And so they went to Bethany, the place where Lazarus was.

When Jesus got to Bethany, he found that Lazarus had already been lying in his grave for four days. Many of the Jewish people had come to Martha and Mary, to comfort them about the death of their brother. When Martha heard that Jesus was coming, she went out and met him, while Mary sat in the house.

"Lord, if you had been here, my brother would not have died," Martha said. "But even now I know that whatever you ask from God, God will give to you." Jesus said to her, "Your brother will rise again."

And Martha said to him, "Yes, I know that he will rise to live again, in the resurrection on the last day."

But Jesus said to her, "I am the resurrection and the life. He who believes in me, even though he dies, will live again. And whoever lives and believes in me shall never die. Do you believe this?"

And Martha said to him, "Yes, Lord, I believe. I believe that you are the Christ, the son of God, who was to come into the world."

And when Martha had said this, she went on her way and called to her sister Mary in secret. She said to her, "The Master has come here and is calling for you." As soon as Mary heard this, she quickly got up and went to meet Jesus. Now, Jesus had not yet come into the village, but was still in the place where Martha had met him. There were Jewish people who were there in the house with Mary to comfort her.

When they saw Mary get up quickly and go out, they followed after her, saying, "She goes to her brother's grave, to weep there."

Then when Mary came to where Jesus was and saw him, she fell down at his feet, saying to him, "Lord, if you had been here, my brother would not have died."

And when Jesus saw her weeping, and the people also weeping who had come with her, he groaned within himself, and he was very troubled. He said, "Where then have you laid him to rest?"

And they said to him, "Lord, come and see."

Jesus wept.

Then the people said, "See how much he loved Lazarus!"

But some others said, "If he could open the eyes of the blind to see again, could he not also have kept this man from dying?"

And then Jesus, groaning in his heart once again, came to the grave of Lazarus. It was a tomb in a cave, and a great stone covered the entrance. Jesus said, "Take away the stone."

Then Martha came forward and said to him, "But he has been dead for four days. By this time there will be a foul smell from the body."

But Jesus said to her, "Did I not say to you before, 'If you will believe, you will see the glory of God?'"

Then they took away the stone from the entrance to the tomb. And then Jesus lifted up his eyes, and he said, "Father, I thank you that you have heard me. I know that you hear me always, but I say this out loud because the people are standing by listening. I say it so that they will believe that you have sent me."

And when Jesus had said these words, he cried out with a loud voice, "Lazarus, come out!" And then the dead man came out of the tomb, and he was wrapped from head to foot in burial clothes, and his face was covered with a cloth. And Jesus said to them, "Take off the face-cloth, and let him go."

Then many of the Jewish people who were there and saw these things now believed in Jesus. But some of them went to the Pharisees, and told them what Jesus had done.

LUKE 10:38–42; JOHN 11:1–46

# JESUS COMES TO BETHANY

When they heard what Jesus had done at Bethany, the Pharisees and the chief priests gathered together in a council. They said, "What should we do? This man does many miracles. If we leave him alone, everyone will believe in him, and the Romans will come and take away our holy place and our nation."

One who was there was Caiaphas, who was the high priest at that time. He said, "You people know nothing. You do not understand that it is better for us if one man dies for all the people, so that our whole nation will not be destroyed." He did not say this on his own, but as high priest that year, he gave the prophecy that Jesus would die for the Jewish nation. This was not just for the one nation in Israel, but for all the children of God scattered abroad, that they might gather together as one. And so from that day on, the chief priests and the Pharisees made plans together to put Jesus to death.

Now, the time for the Passover feast of the Jewish people was near, and many went up from the country to Jerusalem before the Passover, to make themselves pure for the feast. The people were looking around for Jesus and saying to one another as they stood in the temple, "What do you think? Will Jesus come to the feast?" Both the chief priests and the Pharisees had given an order that if anyone knew where Jesus was, he should tell them, so that they could arrest Jesus.

Six days before the Passover feast, Jesus came to Bethany, where Lazarus was. This was the man that Jesus had raised from the dead. There they put on a supper for Jesus. Martha, the sister of Lazarus, served him, and Lazarus was one of those at the table with him. Mary, the other sister of Lazarus, took a pound of expensive ointment. It was made from pure nard, a very costly perfume. With this ointment, she rubbed the feet of Jesus. The whole house was filled with the sweet smell of the ointment.

One of the disciples of Jesus was watching. It was Judas Iscariot, the one who would later betray him. Judas said, "This ointment could be sold for three hundred silver coins. We could take that money and give it to the poor." Judas said this not because he really cared for the poor, but because he was a thief. When he kept the money box, he often stole what was put into it.

Then Jesus said, "Leave her alone. She has saved this ointment for the time of my burial. The poor you will always have with you, but you will not always have me."

MATTHEW 26; MARK 14; JOHN 11, 12

# JESUS ENTERS JERUSALEM

Now Jesus called his twelve disciples together, and he said to them, "We are going up to Jerusalem. There the Son of man will be delivered to the chief priests and the scribes, and they will condemn him to death. They will turn him over to the Gentiles, and they will mock him, and spit on him, and beat him, and kill him. And then on the third day he will rise from the dead."

And when they came near to Jerusalem, they came to Bethphage, to the Mount of Olives. Then Jesus sent two of his disciples ahead, saying to them, "Go into the village you see across from you. As soon as you go there, you will find a donkey tied up, a young colt that has never been ridden. Untie it, and bring it here to me. And if anyone should ask you, 'Why are you doing this?' you will say, 'Because the Lord has need of it.'"

And so the disciples went away, and they did as Jesus had ordered them. They found a colt tied at the door out in the open street, and they untied it. Its owners saw this and said, "What are you doing?"

And so the disciples said what Jesus had told them, "The Lord has need of it." And the owners let them go.

The disciples brought the colt to Jesus, and they put their coats on it, and Jesus sat on it to ride.

And then a great crowd of people who were standing by spread their coats down on the road. Others cut down leafy branches from the palm trees, and spread them in the way. And the crowds went before Jesus, shouting, "Blessed is the King who comes in the name of the Lord! Peace in heaven, and glory to God in the highest!"

And then some of the Pharisees who were with the crowd said to Jesus, "Teacher, correct your disciples! Tell them to be silent!"

Jesus said to them, "Truly I say to you, if these people were silent, then the very stones themselves would cry out."

MATTHEW 20–21; MARK 10–11; LUKE 18–19; JOHN 12

# JESUS CLEARS THE TEMPLE

When Jesus came near Jerusalem, he looked out over the city, and he wept over it. He said, "O, Jerusalem! If you only knew, even today, the things that will bring peace to you! But they are hidden from your eyes. For the days will come upon you, when your enemies will put a wall around you and surround you, and they will close you in on every side. They will bring you down to the ground, and your children with you, and they will not leave one stone standing upon another. This is because you did not know the time of your visit from God."

And then when Jesus came into Jerusalem, all the city was moved, saying, "Who is this?"

And the crowds with him answered and said, "This is Jesus, the prophet from Nazareth of Galilee."

Then Jesus entered the temple of God in Jerusalem. There in the temple he found people who bought and sold things. Some sold oxen and sheep and doves, and others exchanged Roman money for Jewish money.

Jesus made a whip of small cords, and he drove them all out of the temple, with their sheep and their oxen. He poured out the coins of the money-changers, and he turned over their tables. He would not let anyone carry anything through the temple.

Jesus said to them, "Is it not written, 'My house shall be called a house of prayer for all the nations?' But you have made it a den of thieves!"

The chief priests and the scribes heard what Jesus said. And they searched for a way to destroy Jesus, for they feared him. But they could not find a way to do this, because all the people paid attention to his every word.

MATTHEW 21; MARK 11; LUKE 19; JOHN 2

And so the disciples went into the city, and they found things just as Jesus had said. They did what he had told them, and they prepared the Passover meal.

When it was evening and the time for the meal had come, Jesus came to the house with the twelve disciples. He sat down at the table with them.

As they were eating, Jesus said to them, "Truly, truly, I say to you, one of you will betray me, one who is eating with me now."

And the disciples became very troubled, and they said to him one by one, "Is it I? Is it I?"

Jesus answered them and said, "It is one of you twelve here, one who has dipped his bread into the dish with me."

MATTHEW 26; MARK 14; LUKE 22

233

# JESUS TELLS OF HIS DEATH

After Jesus had said, "One of you will betray me," the disciples all began to ask questions among themselves. They wondered which one of them it could be that would betray Jesus.

Then Jesus said to them, "The Son of man will go, as it has been written of him, but woe to that man who betrays the Son of man! It would be better for that person if he had never been born!"

Then Judas, who was the one who betrayed Jesus, said to him, "Master, is it I?"

And Jesus answered, "You have said it."

Jesus said to him, "What you are about to do, do quickly."

Now, no one at the table knew why Jesus said this to him. Because Judas had the money bag, some of them thought that Jesus had said to him, "Buy those things that we need for the feast." Or they thought that perhaps Jesus had said, "Go out and give something to the poor."

And then Judas went out. And it was night.

When Judas had gone out, Jesus said to his disciples, "Now the Son of man is glorified, and God is glorified in him.

"Little children, I will be with you only a little while longer. You will search for me, and just as I told the others, I tell you now: Where I go, you cannot come. And so now I give you a new commandment. Love one another. Just as I have loved you, you must love one another. For in this way all will know that you are my disciples, if you love one another."

And as they were eating, Jesus said, "I have greatly wished to eat this Passover meal with you, before I suffer. For truly I say to you, I will not eat of it again until that day when it becomes true in the kingdom of God."

Then Jesus took the bread, and he gave thanks, and he broke it and gave it to his disciples.

He said to them, "Take this and eat it, all of you. This is my body, which will be given up for you. Do this in memory of me."

And then Jesus took up the cup of wine, and again he gave thanks, and he gave it to his disciples.

He said to them, "Drink from this, all of you. This is my blood, the blood of the new covenant, which will be poured out for you, for the forgiveness of sins.

"For truly I say to you, I will not drink again of the fruit of the vine, until that day when I drink it new in the kingdom of God."

Then they all sang a hymn, and then Jesus went out to the Mount of Olives. His disciples followed after him.

There Jesus said to his disciples, "On this night all of you will fall away on account of me, because it has been written, 'I will strike the shepherd, and the sheep of the flock will be scattered.' But after I have risen again, I will go ahead of you into Galilee."

Then Peter answered and said to him, "Though all others may fall away because of you, I will never fall away." And all the other disciples said the same.

And then Peter said to Jesus, "Lord, where is it that you are going now?"

And Jesus answered Peter and said to him, "Where I go now, you cannot follow. But you shall follow me afterwards."

Peter said to him, "Lord, why do you say that I cannot follow you now? I am ready to go with you, to go to prison, and even to death. I will give up my life for you."

But then Jesus said to Peter, "Will you really give up your life for me? Truly I say to you that on this very night, before the rooster crows in the morning, you will deny that you know me. You will deny me three times."

MATTHEW 26; MARK 14; LUKE 22; JOHN 13

# THE GARDEN OF GETHSEMANE

When Jesus had spoken those words to his disciples, he went out with them over the brook of Kidron. There was a garden there, called the garden of Gethsemane. Jesus and his disciples went into it.

They all knew this place, because Jesus often went there with his disciples. And Judas, the betrayer of Jesus, knew this place also.

Jesus said to his disciples, "Sit here, while I go over there to pray."

Then Jesus took with him Peter, and also James and John, the two sons of Zebedee. Jesus became filled with sorrow, and very troubled. He said to them, "My soul is overcome with sorrow, even to the point of death. Stay here with me and keep watch."

And then Jesus went on a little farther, and he fell to the ground, and he prayed. He said, "O my Father, if it is possible, let the cup pass from me! Nevertheless, I will do not as I wish, but as you wish."

Then Jesus came back to the disciples, and he found that they were sleeping. He said to Peter, "What, are you sleeping? Could you not watch with me for just one hour?"

Jesus said, "Watch and pray, that you do not fall into temptation. For the spirit is willing, but the flesh is weak."

Then Jesus went away from them a second time, and again he prayed. He said, "O my Father, if this cup cannot pass from me unless I drink from it, may your will be done."

And then Jesus came back and he found the disciples asleep again, for their eyes were heavy. And he left them again, and again he went away to pray, and again he said the same words.

Then once more Jesus came back to his disciples, and he said to them, "Sleep on now, and take your rest. The hour is here, when the Son of man will be betrayed into the hands of sinners. For the one who has betrayed me is now near."

MATTHEW 26; MARK 14; LUKE 22; JOHN 18

# JESUS IS CAPTURED

*J*ust then a large band of men came into the garden carrying torches. They were armed with swords and clubs. They had been sent there by the chief priests and the elders of the people. Judas was with them, to lead them to Jesus.

Judas had told them earlier, "I will give you a sign. The one that I will kiss is the man. Take him and arrest him."

Then Judas went up to Jesus at once and he said, "Hail, Master." And then he kissed him.

Jesus said to him, "Friend, why have you come here? Would you betray the Son of man with a kiss?"

Then the men came forward to take hold of Jesus and arrest him. But Peter took out his sword and he struck one of those in the crowd with it. This was a man named Malchus, who was a servant of the high priest. Peter took his sword and cut off the man's right ear.

But Jesus said to him, "No more of this! Put your sword back in its place. All those who take up the sword will die by the sword." And Jesus touched the man's ear and healed him.

Then Jesus said, "Do you not know that I could now pray to my Father, and he would at once send me more than twelve armies of angels? But how then would the writings of the prophets come true, that say it must happen in this way?"

Jesus said to the crowd, "Do you come to me now as if I were a thief, with swords and clubs to take me? Every day I sat teaching with you in the temple, and not one of you put his hand on me then. But now it is your time, the hour when darkness rules. All this has happened, so that the words of the prophets might come true."

Then all the disciples left Jesus, and they ran away.

MATTHEW 26; MARK 14; LUKE 22; JOHN 18

# JESUS IS PUT ON TRIAL

So the crowd took hold of Jesus and they arrested him. They tied him up, and they led him away from the garden. They took him to the palace of Caiaphas, the high priest. The chief priests and the scribes and the elders had all gathered there to put Jesus on trial.

The chief priests and the scribes and the elders all tried to find witnesses who would speak falsely against Jesus, so that they could put him to death. But they found none.

Then finally two false witnesses came forward. They said, "We have heard Jesus say, 'I can destroy the temple of God, and then build it back up again in just three days.'"

Then the high priest got up and he said to Jesus, "Have you no answer to this? What do you say to these charges made against you?"

But Jesus was silent, and he gave no answer.

Then the high priest said to Jesus, "I order you now, by the power of the living God, tell us this: Are you are the Christ, the Son of God?"

And Jesus said to him, "I am. It is just as you have said. But now I say to you: After this you will see the Son of man seated at the right hand of God the Almighty, and coming on the clouds of heaven."

Then the high priest tore his clothes in anger, saying, "His words are a crime against God! What need do we have for more witnesses now? Listen, everyone, you have heard his crime in his own words!"

Then the high priest turned to the people and he said, "What do you think now?"

And the people answered him and said, "He is guilty. He deserves to be killed."

Then they blindfolded Jesus, and they began to hit him. They spit in his face, and they slapped him with their hands. They mocked him and said, "Tell us now, O Christ. You are the great prophet. Who is it that just hit you?"

MATTHEW 26; MARK 14; LUKE 22; JOHN 18

# PETER DENIES JESUS

Peter had followed far behind the crowd as they took Jesus to the high priest's palace. He stopped outside the door of the palace and sat down with the servants, as he waited to see what would happen to Jesus.

The servants had made a fire in the courtyard, for it was cold. They were standing by the fire, and Peter was there with them also, warming himself by the fire. Then a young servant girl came up, and she saw Peter sitting there in the firelight. The girl looked carefully at him and said, "You were there. You were in the garden with Jesus of Galilee."

But he denied this, saying to her, "I do not know what you mean."

Then Peter went outside. There the girl saw him again. She said to those who were standing by, "This man was there. He was with Jesus."

Again Peter denied this, saying, "I swear I do not know the man."

And then after a while the people who were standing by came up to Peter and they said, "You must be one of those with Jesus, because you speak like someone from Galilee. Your accent gives you away."

Peter began to curse and swear, saying, "I do not know the man!" Just then a rooster crowed.

Then Peter remembered the words of Jesus. He had said to him, "Before the rooster crows, you will deny me three times." And Peter went away, and he wept bitterly.

MATTHEW 26; MARK 14; LUKE 22; JOHN 18

# JESUS IS BROUGHT TO PILATE

*T*hen it was morning. Judas, who had betrayed Jesus, now saw that Jesus had been condemned. Judas was sorry for what he had done, and he went to the chief priests and the elders. He took with him the thirty large silver coins that they had paid him to betray Jesus, so that he could give the money back.

Judas said to them, "I have sinned. I have betrayed the innocent blood."

And they answered Judas and said to him, "What is that to us? You must see to that yourself."

Then Judas threw down the thirty silver shekels in the temple. He left the temple, and he went away and hanged himself.

Then the chief priests picked up the thirty silver coins that Judas had left behind. They said, "It is against our law to put this money into the treasury. This is blood money."

And so they all met together. They decided to use the money to buy the potter's field, to use it as a place for burying poor strangers. And so this field came to be called the Field of Blood, and it is still called that even today.

Then as soon as the morning had come, all the chief priests held a meeting with the scribes and the elders of the people. They decided together that Jesus should be put to death. And so they tied Jesus up and they led him away from the palace of Caiaphas. They turned him over to Pontius Pilate.

They brought Jesus to the hall of judgment of Pilate, who was the Roman governor. And Pilate said to them, "What charge do you make against this man?"

MATTHEW 27; MARK 15; LUKE 23; JOHN 18

# JESUS IS ACCUSED

And so they began to accuse Jesus, saying, "This man is trying to ruin our nation. He is against paying taxes to Caesar, and he says that he himself is Christ the king."

They also accused Jesus by saying, "He stirs up the people by his teaching, in all parts of Judea. He began in Galilee, and he has now come to this place here."

Then Pilate called Jesus to come before him, and he said to him, "Are you the king of the Jews?"

Jesus answered him, "Do you ask me this yourself, or do you ask it because others have said this about me?"

Pilate answered him, "Am I a Jew? Your own people and the chief priests have brought you to me. What have you done?"

Jesus answered, "My kingdom is not of this world. If my kingdom were of this world, then my followers would fight, so that I could not be arrested. But my kingdom is not of this present world."

And so Pilate said to him, "Then you are a king!"

Jesus said to him, "You have said so. You say that I am a king, by your question. This is what I say: For this reason I was born, and for this cause I came into the world, to give witness to the truth. Everyone who is for the truth will hear my voice."

And Pilate said to him, "What is truth?"

Then Jesus was accused of many other things by the chief priests and the elders. But he gave no answer in his own defense.

Pilate then said to him, "Do you not hear how many things they say against you? Have you nothing to say in answer?"

But still Jesus did not answer. He did not say even one word. And Pilate was greatly amazed at this.

MATTHEW 27; MARK 15; LUKE 23; JOHN 18

# GIVE US BARABBAS!

Now in those days there was a certain custom. At the time of the Passover feast, the Roman governor would release one prisoner. The people could choose whichever prisoner they wanted, and that person would be set free.

Now there was in the prison a certain notorious prisoner, called Barabbas. He was a thief and a murderer, and he had taken part in a rebellion in the city.

And so on that morning a crowd of people came together, and they called out to Pilate to do what he had done before, and set one prisoner free.

Pilate the governor said to them, "Which man should I release to you: Barabbas, or Jesus, the one who is called the Christ?"

# JESUS IS BURIED

When Jesus gave up his spirit and died, just at that moment the curtain of the temple was torn in two by a great wind, all the way from the top to the bottom. The earth shook with an earthquake, and the rocks were split. The tombs broke open, and the bodies of many holy people who had died were brought back to life. They came out of their tombs, and after the resurrection of Jesus they went out into the holy city of Jerusalem. There they were seen by many people.

A Roman officer who was there at the cross with Jesus saw this earthquake, and all the things that had happened. The Roman officer said, "Truly this man was the Son of God."

Some women were also there, watching from a distance. They had followed Jesus out from Jerusalem to care for his needs. Among them were Mary Magdalene, Mary who was the mother of James and Joses, and Mary the wife of Zebedee and mother of James and John.

It was then the day before the sabbath. When the evening came, a follower of Jesus came forward, a man named Joseph from the Judean town of Arimathea. He was a member of the council, but he had not agreed to their decision and their action. Joseph was a good and fair man, and he was waiting for the kingdom of God.

Joseph went in bravely to Pontius Pilate, and he asked for the body of Jesus. Pilate ordered that the body be given over to Joseph.

And Joseph brought a fine linen cloth, and he took down the body of Jesus from the cross. He wrapped it in the linen cloth. He laid the body to rest in his own new tomb, which he had carved out from a rock.

Joseph had a huge stone rolled in front of the entrance to the tomb, and then he went away. Mary Magdalene and the other Mary, the mother of Joses, were there. They were watching as this was done.

MATTHEW 27:51–61; MARK 15:38–41; LUKE 23:47–55; JOHN 19:31–42

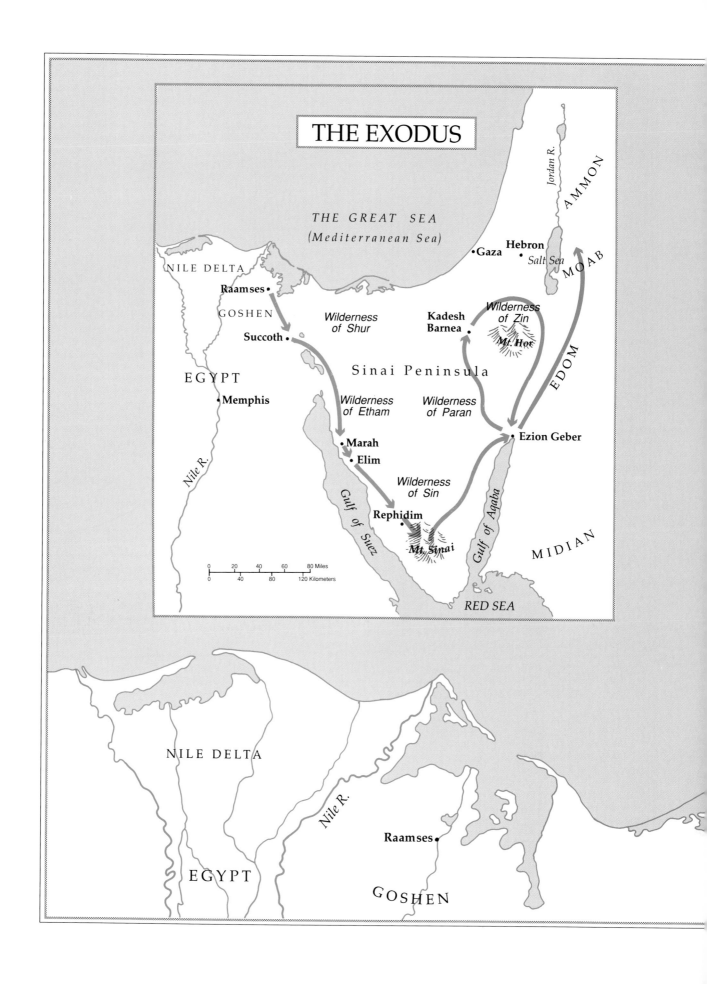

# THE EXODUS

*THE GREAT SEA*
*(Mediterranean Sea)*

*Jordan R.*

AMMON

MOAB

EDOM

MIDIAN

NILE DELTA

Raamses•

GOSHEN

•Gaza    **Hebron**
         •*Salt Sea*

Succoth•

*Wilderness
of Shur*

**Kadesh
Barnea**•

*Wilderness
of Zin*

*Mt. Hor*

S i n a i   P e n i n s u l a

**EGYPT**

•**Memphis**

*Wilderness
of Etham*

*Wilderness
of Paran*

*Gulf of Suez*

*Gulf of Aqaba*

•**Marah**
•**Elim**

*Wilderness
of Sin*

**Rephidim**•

*Mt. Sinai*

•**Ezion Geber**

*Nile R.*

| 0 | 20 | 40 | 60 | 80 Miles |
|---|---|---|---|---|
| 0 | 40 | 80 | | 120 Kilometers |

*RED SEA*

NILE DELTA

*Nile R.*

**Raamses**•

**EGYPT**

GOSHEN

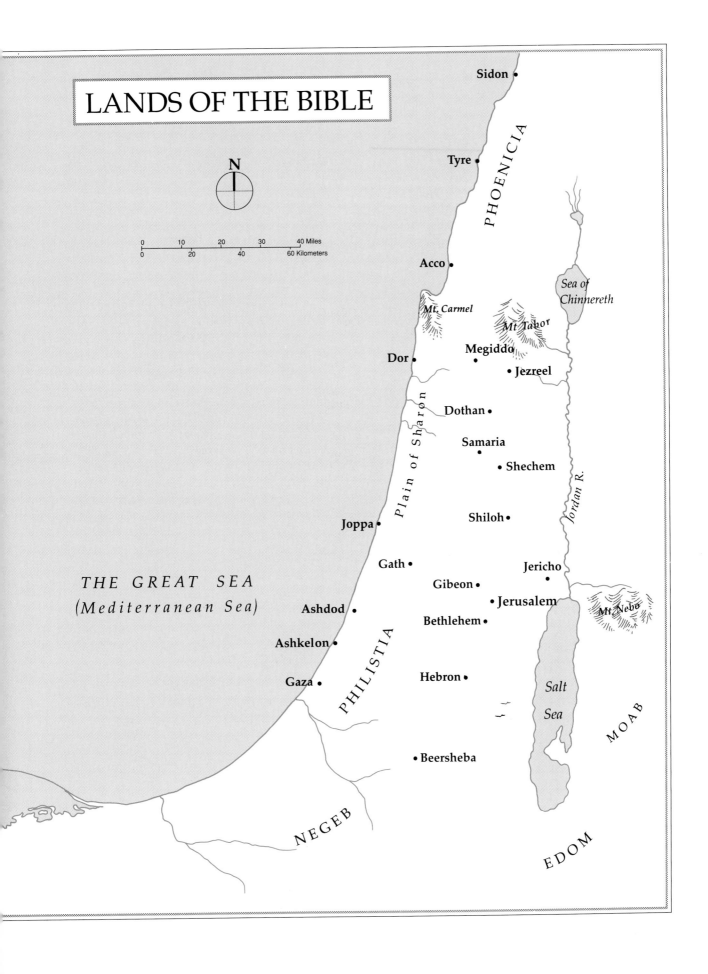

# LANDS OF THE BIBLE

N

| 0 | 10 | 20 | 30 | 40 Miles |
| 0 | 20 | 40 | 60 Kilometers |

Sidon •

PHOENICIA

Tyre •

Acco •

*Mt. Carmel*

Sea of
*Chinnereth*

*Mt Tabor*

Megiddo •

Dor • • Jezreel

*Plain of Sharon*

Dothan •

Samaria •

• Shechem

*Jordan R.*

Shiloh •

Joppa •

Gath • Jericho •

Gibeon •

*Mt Nebo*

Ashdod • • Jerusalem

Ashkelon • Bethlehem •

PHILISTIA

Hebron •

Gaza • *Salt Sea*

*THE GREAT SEA*
*(Mediterranean Sea)*

MOAB

• Beersheba

NEGEB

EDOM

# GEOGRAPHY OF THE HOLY LAND

The Holy Land does not have a single type of geography. The landscape changes from flat coastal plains to high mountains to valleys that lie well below sea level. This differing geography fits into a small area that measures only about 150 miles from north to south, running from Dan to Beersheba.

The Holy Land is surrounded by great natural barriers. The Mediterranean Sea (called the Great Sea in ancient times) lies to the west. There are high mountains to the north and vast, empty desert areas to the south and the east.

## Deserts and Farmland

The soil of the land of Israel varied greatly, from desert regions that supported only shepherds and tribes of nomads, to fertile regions in which there were many productive farmlands. Even today, the change in the terrain from farmland to desert is obvious as one moves inland from the seacoast. The prevailing west-to-east winds pick up moisture from the Mediterranean and then lose it in the form of rain as they rise upward to the highlands. As the now-dry winds descend into the Jordan valley, the lack of rainfall there creates the desert areas.

The land of Israel is also on the border of two climate zones, the Mediterranean and the Sahara-Arabian, so that any change in the landscape causes a marked change in the climate. In the winter, the Mediterranean climate brings rain, while the Sahara-Arabian climate remains dry. The winds from the west pass over the Mediterranean, bringing rain, while winds from the south blow over dry land and, thus do not bring rain. Although the average rainfall in Biblical times has been calculated at about ten inches per year, more than twenty inches might fall in the north, with less than two inches in the south.

## The Coastal Plain

Around the southern end of the Holy Land near Gaza, the coastal strip of land along the Mediterranean is about twelve and one-half miles wide. Here, near the open sea, the land has many natural springs and it is covered with vegetation, including fruit and sycamore trees.

Just north of this area, great sand dunes, reaching heights of 150 feet, cut off a rolling, treeless plain from the sea. Running along the east side of this plain a row of low foothills, called the Shephelah in the Bible, extend to the mountainous region of Judah.

Farther north there is a fertile region that in Biblical times could be easily reached from the chief city of Jerusalem. Above this region is the Plain of Sharon, which was covered with wooded areas and served as grazing land for sheep and goats sent down from the high country when vegetation was scarce.

As it continues north, this strip narrows and is only about two miles wide at the ancient city of Caesarea. Somewhat north of this point, the coastal plains are interrupted by the Carmel range, which extends out to the very edge of the sea. Beyond the mountains, the plains again pick up, forming the Bay of Acre. The Biblical city of Acco was located here, surrounded by the fertile and well-populated plain of Acre. A bit farther north on this same narrow strip lay the ancient city of Tyre, not far below the northern boundary of the Holy Land.

Even with its long shoreline, this area has a lack of natural harbors, and so Israel never developed as a seagoing nation.

## The Highlands

The high country of the Holy Land is bordered on the south by the desert region of the Negev, which literally means "parched country." The low hills of the Shephelah extend from the coastal plain to the mountainous ridge, which runs lengthwise through the center of the region.

The settlements in this region were protected from surprise attack by the high elevation and the rough terrain. Securely perched high in the mountains, they overlooked the coastal plain to the west and the great valley to the east. Hebron, one of the southernmost settlements, is 3,000 feet above sea level. Because of its central location and position in the mountains, King David chose Jerusalem as his capital city.

Northward, the land opens to the valleys of Samaria, which are less than 600 feet above sea level. Mount Gerizim, a sacred high place of the Samaritans, rises above the valley at a height of 2,800 feet. Shechem lies in the pass between it and Mount Ebal to the north, which rises to 3,120 feet. This pass forms a sharp division between northern and southern Samaria.

At this point the Carmel ridge turns west into the Mediterranean Sea. Along the northeastern edge of this ridge is the Plain of Esdraelon; its western region is known as the Plain of Megiddo and the eastern section as the Plain of Jezreel. This triangular-shaped plain, 200 feet above sea level, is the most fertile area in all of the Holy Land.

To the north lies the region of Galilee. The lower portion of this area, which slopes up from the Plain of Esdraelon, is known as "Lower Galilee," and the land continuing to rise up toward Syria is "Upper Galilee." The mountains in Galilee are high, reaching elevations of about 4,000 feet. The highlands keep rising into Lebanon, where the snow-covered cap of Mount Hermon reaches 9,700 feet above sea level.

At the most northern point in Galilee, the mountains drop abruptly to the Jordan valley on the east. The streams of the region of Lower Galilee lead into the Sea of Galilee, with Mount Tabor on the southeastern corner providing a view over the entire region.

## The Great Rift Valley

A great rift, or opening, divides the Holy Land lengthwise into two sections. It is the deepest ditch on the face of the earth. It is part of a huge fault that runs some 350 miles, from the mountains of Lebanon in the north to the Gulf of Aqaba in the south. This rift, called "the Ghor" or "the valley," is 1,268 feet below sea level at its greatest depth, and the highlands drop steeply to it from elevations of 3,000 feet.

The Jordan River, fed by streams from Mount Hermon, runs through the Great Rift, falling about nine feet with each mile that it flows. The Jordan River ends in the Dead Sea to the south. The river supplies water for the lakes along its path, including the Sea of Galilee (Lake Galilee). This heart-shaped body of fresh water is thirteen miles long and is eight miles wide at its widest point. Its surface lies 680 feet below sea level. The land is marshy where the Jordan River enters the lake. A strip of land on the northwestern shore of the lake was known as the Plain of Ginnesar in the time of Jesus, and the lake itself is called the Lake of Chinnereth in the Old Testament.

It is 65 miles from the Sea of Galilee to the Dead Sea, but the Jordan loops and twists almost 200 miles to travel this distance. The Great Rift widens below the Sea of Galilee from a beginning of about four miles to a width of thirteen to fourteen miles. At the bottom of this broad section is a deep depression of one hundred or more feet that is the actual river bottom. Gray hills still cover the slopes leading to the lower level, and the depression itself was once covered by jungle-like plant growth, which provided a home for many wild animals. This area is called "the Zor" or "thicket."

As the Rift continues southward, the river bottom narrows and vegetation decreases, for rainfall is rare in this area and little water seeps down from the parched western slopes of the highlands. There are oases in this region, however, including one with a great spring near which one of the oldest cities on earth, the Biblical Jericho, was settled.

The Jordan River ends in the Dead Sea, its incoming waters taken up by the hot sun and dry air of the region. The water of the Dead Sea is so salty that a person will not sink in it, and its Hebrew name is literally "Sea of Salt." It is 53 miles long and nine to ten feet wide, and it lies 1,286 feet below sea level. The water level is as deep as 1,300 feet, although in Biblical times one could wade across the southern part. From the southern end of the Dead Sea, the Rift continues for another 100 miles to the Gulf of Aqaba.

# BIBLICAL PLANTS AND ANIMALS

The Holy Land of Biblical times covered an area that had different amounts of rainfall and different kinds of soil in various places. This meant that many different kinds of plants grew in the different regions.

## The Natural Plant Life

Along the coast of the Great Sea (Mediterranean Sea) lay the marshy soil of Sharon and parts of Esdraelon, with some areas covered by forest. The land of the Philistines had few trees, except in the valley bottoms. But up the coast to the north, groves of sycamore trees covered the land.

The hill country of Judah and Samaria was covered with thick oak and pine forests. The plant growth was thicker on the northern and western slopes, where the rainfall was greater and the evaporation less than on the eastern and southern slopes.

A ground cover of scrub woodland and shrubs stretched into the semidesert area, extending into what is now Jordan. The western slopes of the hills of Galilee were rich with trees and vegetation. Along with the pine forests, there were hawthorns, plantains, and wild pear trees. The country to the south and east of the highlands was covered with grass. The hills of the desert areas were often barren, but the wadis (gullies or stream beds) had a thin line of saltbush and tamarisk. In the Great Rift Valley, low-lying areas with enough heat and moisture became marshes that were almost impossible to cross. Tropical plants such as papyrus and doum palms grew there, with tamarisk jungle in the flood plain of the Jordan River.

## The Crops

As people cleared away the old wild plant growth, they planted farm crops. In place of forest trees, they grew olives; in place of the scrub woodland, they planted grape vines; and in place of the grasses, they grew grains, such as wheat and barley. In the Bible, these crops are often mentioned together because they provided the basic needs of the people.

The Bible also speaks of the food known as pulse (lentils, peas, and beans) that was an important part of the people's diet. Jacob bought his brother Esau's birthright with pottage, a stew made of pulse. And even though they were threatened by King Nebuchadnezzar of Babylon, Daniel and his companions chose to eat pulse instead of the daily provision of the king's meat.

Grain was grown between the olive trees, and pulse between the grape vines. Together these crops provided a well-balanced diet that a farmer could raise with the help of only his family, and he would consider himself fortunate to have this food.

The Promised Land in which the Israelites had settled was rich and fruitful, and it provided the people with more than simply the necessities of their everyday lives. In the summer there were also foods that were considered by the people to be special treats, such as figs, pomegranates, and spices and nuts:

*One basket had very good figs, like first-ripe figs. (Jeremiah 24:2)*

*Your shoots are an orchard of pomegranates with all choicest fruits. (Song of Solomon 4:13)*

*. . . carry down to the man a present, a little balm and a little honey, gum, myrrh, pistachio nuts, and almonds. (Genesis 43:11)*

## The Wild Animals

But the Promised Land could also be dangerous. Wild animals such as lions, bears, wolves, jackals, and hyenas were a danger to farm animals, or even to people, who wandered too far from their villages or farms. These wild animals were a constant threat to the flocks of sheep:

*David said to Saul, "Your servant used to keep sheep for his father; and when there came a lion, or a bear, and took a lamb from the flock, I went after him and smote him." (1 Samuel 17:34)*

266

Although the people feared the mighty lion, they also respected its courage and strength:

*The lion, which is mightiest among beasts and does not turn back before any. (Proverbs 30:30)*

There were many snakes and reptiles found in the land, such as cobras, asps, adders, green lizards and monitor lizards, and white geckos or gray geckos. Some of these snakes were poisonous.

In the rivers and lakes of the Holy Land, carp, catfish, and other fish lived along with the hippopotamus and the crocodile. It may be that these two animals were the two large beasts mentioned in the Bible, the "behemoth" (hippopotamus) and the "leviathan" (crocodile).

Birds of all kinds were in the land, those that could fly and those that could not. Many were birds of prey, such as the eagle and the hawk.

The forests, the plains, and the desert were full of game animals that the people could hunt. King Solomon's table was provided with "harts, gazelles, roebucks, and fatted fowl." (1 Kings 4:23). In addition to those the people had already tamed, wild goats and asses roamed the hills and plains.

There were also many insects in the land of the Bible, including bees, which were the source of honey. Lice, flies, grasshoppers, wasps, and locusts were there along with hundreds of kinds of butterflies and beetles. Some insects were eaten, but others, such as the centipede and the scorpion, the Israelites were forbidden to eat:

*Yet among the winged insects that go on all fours you may eat those which have legs above their feet, with which to leap on the earth;*

*Of them you may eat: the locust according to its kind, the bald locust according to its kind, the cricket according to its kind, and the grasshopper according to its kind.*

*But all other winged insects which have four feet are an abomination to you. (Leviticus 11:21–23)*

## The Domesticated Animals

The people of Israel depended upon their flocks of goats and sheep as well as on their crops for food. The sheep were a fat-tailed variety that provided milk, meat, and wool. They were also the source of sheepskin coats that protected the shepherds against the cold. These sheep were highly valued and were often offered in sacrifice.

Goats were raised together with the sheep, even though they were able to range farther into the desert. They also provided meat and milk, and their coarse hair was used to make the heavy cloth for tents. It may be that sheep dogs were used. But it seems that for the most part the Israelites did not think of dogs as pets or work animals.

By the time the kings ruled in Israel, the camel had become the major means of transport in the desert. Its speed and endurance enabled desert tribes, such as the Midianites, to make sudden raids upon the farms and villages of the Israelites, laying waste the land.

The ass, the mule, and the ox were the main work animals of the shepherds and the farmers. Almost every family had an ass or a donkey. These large animals worked hard and could easily travel 25 miles in a day.

The ox was prized most highly. The farmer used it to plow the heavy soil and as a beast of burden. The nomads used oxen to transport all their goods and to carry women and children.

Horses were not common and were considered by the Israelites primarily as animals of war. The chariots of the Egyptians who pursued the people of Israel were pulled by horses. They were also included on the list of animals the Jews brought with them on their return from exile in Babylon. Always the horse was spoken of with great admiration.

*Do you give the horse his might? Do you clothe his neck with strength?*

*Do you make him leap like the locust? His majestic snorting is terrible.*

*He paws in the valley, and exults in his strength; he goes out to meet the weapons. (Job 39:19–22)*

267

# ANCIENT EGYPT

At the time that Abraham, Isaac, and Jacob lived, Egypt had been a powerful country for well over a thousand years. For a time, Egypt was overrun by foreign invaders and its power declined. But, during what historians call The New Kingdom, which dates from about the year 1500 B.C., Egypt became the world's strongest nation. King Thutmose III brought Palestine and Syria into the Egyptian empire and established control over Nubia and Kush.

## The Nile River

Almost from its beginning, this country along the Nile grew in numbers and strength. Extending the length of the land, the river provided a means of transportation and communication for the settlements along its banks. The river also made farming possible.

The Nile River flooded sometime in July each year. In September, the flood waters would recede, leaving a layer of rich, fertile soil (alluvium). This flood area was very hot and dry, with little rainfall.

In spite of the dry climate, crops could be planted with confidence because of the regularity of the Nile's flooding pattern. The people created extensive irrigation systems to water the crops, which made it possible for the land to support a large population.

The fertile land was planted with wheat, barley, and rye. Bread was made from the wheat and a thick beer from the barley. All the grains were important in feeding both the people and their livestock. Grain was stored in granaries in the cities for use in times of famine. Overseers recorded the amount of grain that was put in and taken out:

> *And that food shall be for store to the land against the seven years of famine, which shall be in the land of Egypt. (Genesis 41:36)*

It was so important that provisions be made for times of famine that one-fifth of the produce was given to the Egyptian ruler, the Pharaoh, for distribution in times of need:

> *And it shall come to pass in the increase, that ye shall give the fifth part unto Pharaoh, and four parts shall be your own, for seed of the field, and for your food, and for them of your households, and for food for your little ones. (Genesis 47:24)*

Many kinds of vegetables and fruits, such as dates, figs, and pomegranates, grew in the rich soil. The people were able to catch fish from the Nile, as well as the ducks and geese that lived there. Their cattle furnished them with milk, cheese, and butter. Wealthy Egyptians regularly ate beef or the meat of gazelles and antelopes. They also had fancy baked goods and drank grape, date, or palm wines.

Flax was also raised and was made into linen. In the hot climate, cool linen garments were worn by both men and women, and some of the yarn was used for trading.

The farmer was respected far above the shepherd in Egypt, and few people wanted to tend the flocks. When Joseph's family came to Egypt, he instructed them to tell Pharaoh that they were shepherds, so they would be sent to settle on the grasslands of Goshen:

> *And it shall come to pass, when Pharaoh shall call you, and shall say, "What is your occupation?"*
>
> *That ye shall say, "Thy servants' trade hath been about cattle from our youth even until now, both we, and also our fathers: that ye may dwell in the land of Goshen: for every shepherd is an abomination unto the Egyptians." (Genesis 46:33–34)*

## The Pharaoh

The Egyptians believed that the visible world had been created by divine forces out of a watery waste. These forces also brought into existence the gods who governed every aspect of human life. So, the people of Egypt worshiped many gods. The farmers relied on Re, the sun god, and the goddess Rennutet for their good harvests. Isis ruled with her husband and brother, Osiris, over plant life and the dead. Their son, Horus, was the sky god.

The people of each city and town of ancient Egypt also worshipped their own god as well as the major gods. The great city of Memphis had a creator god called Ptah. The people of Thebes worshipped the sun god Amon. The gods were often pictured as animals or as humans with animal heads.

The king of Egypt lived in a Great House, which was called a Per-ao (or Pharaoh in Hebrew), which gives us his title. Pharaoh was considered to be a god on earth. He assured the rise of the Nile, which in turn assured the prosperity, peace, and order of the land. The Pharaoh was an absolute ruler, and his will became reality as soon as it was spoken. The Egyptians recognized no power on earth greater than his.

But one person alone could not rule such a great empire, and the Pharaoh needed help in governing as the god-king. To the priests fell the care of the temples, which gave them great power. Viziers and governors were appointed by the Pharaoh to aid him in running the country. Joseph was one:

*Thou shalt be over my house, and according unto thy word shall all my people be ruled: only in the throne will I be greater than thou. (Genesis 41:40)*

The Pharaoh also had a large army of foot soldiers and charioteers. Although horses were not originally found in Egypt, they were later brought in from other countries to pull the chariots. Later the Egyptians raised horses themselves.

## The Afterlife

According to the Egyptians, a person's soul or spirit consisted of three parts: *akh* was the part of a person that became an "excellent spirit" and traveled through the floor of the burial chamber to the underworld; *ka* was the exact double of a person (the "shadow" or "name") to which funerary offerings were made; and *ba* was the manifestation of the soul that could enter or leave the dead body.

The Egyptians loved life so much that they wanted to enjoy it even after death. The inscriptions, paintings, and furniture in the tombs were put there for the enjoyment of the dead in the afterlife. This desire also led to the practice of embalming bodies by a process called mummification:

*So Joseph died, being an hundred and ten years old: and they embalmed him and he was put in a coffin in Egypt. (Genesis 50:26)*

The huge pyramids of Egypt were built as tombs for the pharaohs. The oldest one still standing is the pyramid of Zoser, which was built around 2700 B.C. The Great Pyramid of King Khufu at Giza is probably the most famous. It originally stood about 480 feet high and covered 275 square yards. The base is almost precisely aligned with the points of the compass, and its elevation does not vary more than one half inch. It was made of over 2,300,000 huge stone blocks, some weighing as much as 33,000 pounds. The stones were not joined with any type of mortar, but dressed to fit together so perfectly that even something so thin as a piece of paper cannot be slipped between them.

Structures such as the pyramids and the great cities of Egypt required many thousands of workers to construct them.

*Therefore they did set over them taskmasters to afflict them with their burdens. And they built for Pharaoh treasure cities, Pithom and Raamses. (Exodus 1:11)*

During the time the fields were flooded, the farm workers could help in the building. But slaves were needed in addition to the farmers and the skilled craftsmen. These slaves were taken in battle or bought from traders or merchants.

In spite of their mighty position in the ancient world, the people of Egypt seemed to have been cheerful and brooded very little about the place of man before the gods. Life was relatively sure and peaceful for these inhabitants of one of the earliest civilized kingdoms on the earth.

269

# THE ROMAN EMPIRE

The events of the New Testament took place during the time that Palestine was a Roman province. In most of their provinces, including Palestine, the Romans allowed the local authorities to run the government.

At this time, the Roman armies were already moving toward Palestine. Then the Roman general Pompey was invited there to settle a dispute between Hyrcanus II and Aristobulus II, who both wanted to be high priest. Pompey decided in favor of Hyrcanus, and Aristobulus was taken as a prisoner to Rome. Palestine was established as a protectorate, which meant the Jewish state had to pay taxes to Rome.

## The Decapolis

The province of Judea contained ten Hellenistic (Greek) cities that had been built in Palestine by settlers from Greece. Pompey freed these cities from the province, and they became nearly independent under the supervision of the Roman province of Syria. Their culture was non-Jewish. The citizens were content with Roman rule, even though they were still subject to taxation by Rome and were responsible for their own defense. These "ten cities" or Decapolis formed their own federation.

## The Taxes

At the time of Jesus' birth, Palestine was a Roman protectorate governed by Herod I, known as Herod the Great. Herod was an Idumaean (Edomite) whose country had been converted to Judaism about 125 B.C. Herod ruled as king and allowed the high priest to retain his position. The people were required to pay taxes to Herod's royal treasury, as well as a tribute to Rome. This tribute consisted of a tax on land, a poll tax, a tax on personal property, and customs duties. In addition, citizens of Jerusalem were required to pay a house tax, and all Jews had to make an annual payment to the Temple in Jerusalem. An enrollment or census was taken in order to set up future taxation.

*In those days a decree went out from Caesar Augustus that all the world should be enrolled. This was the first enrollment, when Quirinius was governor of Syria.*

*And all went to be enrolled, each to his own city. (Luke 2:1, 3)*

## The Roman Prefect

At the time that Jesus set out to bring his message to the people, Palestine was governed by two men:

*In the fifteenth year of the reign of Tiberius Caesar, Pontius Pilate being governor of Judaea, and Herod being tetrarch of Galilee . . . (Luke 3:1)*

The Herod mentioned in this verse is the son of Herod the Great, Herod Antipas, who was the tetrarch, or governor, of Galilee and Perea.

As a Roman prefect, or governor, Pontius Pilate was responsible for collecting the revenues, ensuring the peace and stability of the province, and conducting trials that involved crimes punishable by death.

Since Pilate was the prefect of Judaea, it was also necessary for him to work with the Sanhedrin (a council of scribes, elders, and priests) and the high priest. The high priest of Judaea at this time was Caiaphas.

## Roman Religion

The Roman government controlled their own religion. Their priests were government officials, who were elected or appointed. They performed public ceremonies to win the favor of the gods for the state. This meant that religious ceremonies included expressions of patriotism. The Romans thought that strong feeling was out of place in acts of worship. Their attitude toward religion, both their own religion and that of others, was very tolerant. So long as a Roman performed the proper religious actions, he was free to think what he liked about the gods.

The early Romans worshipped city gods and gods who performed certain functions, such as Janus who guarded their doors, and Vesta, the goddess of the home and hearth, in addition to the high gods, such as Jupiter, the sky god, and Mars, who protected them in war. The ceremonial rites usually involved a sacrifice accompanied by a prayer or vow. Pigs were the most common animal sacrifice, with sheep and oxen reserved for more important occasions.

In Palestine, the Jews were not forced to take part in the worship of Roman gods. They were allowed to worship God under their own priests and according to their own traditions.

*Now his parents went to Jerusalem every year at the feast of the Passover.*

*And when he was twelve years old, they went up according to custom . . . (Luke 2:41–42)*

## The Roman Army

There were about 3,000 Roman soldiers stationed in Judaea. Their headquarters were in Caesarea, a city built by Herod the Great. The soldiers manned the smaller forts, policed the roads and ports, and oversaw the collection of taxes. They also helped to build and repair roads and bridges.

The Roman army was made up of troops of Roman citizens and also auxiliary troops recruited among the people of areas conquered by Rome. The army in Palestine consisted mainly of these auxiliary troops. The Jews did not have to serve in these auxiliary forces.

The legion was the basic unit of the Roman army. Its size varied from 3,000 to 6,000 men, who were commanded by a legate. The legion was divided into ten cohorts, each commanded by a professional soldier called a tribune. A cohort was composed of six centuries, each commanded by a centurion. Although most centurions were Roman citizens, a non-Roman could rise through the ranks of the auxiliary troops to that level. This meant that centurions were thoroughly tested fighting men who were able to command others.

## The Communities in the Empire

The Jewish communities in Rome and its provinces were, on the whole, recognized and tolerated by the Roman authorities. The Jewish people were not required to live in ghettos (separate living areas for Jews only), as they were in Europe in later times. Many of them lived in the Roman manner. The inhabitants of many cities of the empire were given the rights of Roman citizens. Tarsus in Cilicia, the home of Saul who became the Apostle Paul, was such a city; this may have been why he qualified as a citizen of Rome. At one time, it was even possible to buy citizenship.

*When the centurion heard that, he went to the tribune and said to him, "What are you about to do? For this man is a Roman citizen."*

*So the tribune came and said to him, "Tell me, are you a Roman citizen?" And he said, "Yes."*

*The tribune answered, "I bought this citizenship for a large sum." Paul said, "But I was born a citizen." (Acts 22:26–28)*

## The Crucifixion

According to Jewish law, the Sanhedrin, which was the supreme Jewish court, could not condemn a man to death at night, nor could they meet during the Passover holiday. Although the arrest of Jesus took place the night of the Passover feast, some members of the Sanhedrin questioned Jesus anyway.

Jesus was then taken to Pontius Pilate. It was the policy of Rome not to interfere with religious matters brought before the local authorities. But Pilate did have authority if the crime was against Rome or if it resulted in a civil disturbance.

The Romans often used crucifixion as a form of execution, particularly for the lowest criminals. Jesus died on a cross at Golgotha, between the crosses of two thieves.

*Then Jesus, crying with a loud voice, said, "Father, into thy hands I commit my spirit!" And having said this, he breathed his last. (Luke 23:46).*

271

# LIFE IN THE TIME OF JESUS

During the time of Jesus, most of the people of the Holy Land lived in small villages, often close to a larger town. The towns were surrounded by walls behind which the people could shelter in times of danger, and an open space in front of the town gates served as a market, a gathering place, and as a court.

## The Home

The house was the center of family life, and a courtyard formed an important part of most of the houses. A typical village house was often no more than a white-washed cube, usually made of clay, brick, or woven sticks and branches, with a door and perhaps a few other openings. The inside was made up only of a single room. This room was divided in two parts, one for the family and one for the family's animals, who actually lived inside the house.

Wealthier families built their homes around a center court with small rooms opening on to it. There were no separate kitchens except in the houses of the very rich. The cooking was done in the courtyard or in a lean-to if the weather was bad.

Most houses had a flat roof surrounded by a low wall with a staircase, usually outside the house, leading up to it. On the roof, clothing was dried and tools were stored. Often the family gathered on the roof in the evening and slept there on warm summer nights. The men also used the roof to pray and meditate. Wealthier people often set a light building on the roof, and this gradually turned into a second story or "upper room" used to house overnight guests or serve a large dinner party. This is the type of room in which the Last Supper was eaten.

Furniture was simple, and the most important single piece was the chest. Chests were used for provisions and for clothing. Poor families ate their meals on the chest, or on a grain-measure turned upside down. Those who were better off had tables; stools and chairs of cloth or woven straw on a wooden frame were also used. Some people had beds with cushions, blankets, and a head-rest to support the neck. Poorer people stacked mats in the living room or on the roof, rolling themselves in their cloaks and using a piece of wood or a stone for a pillow. The very wealthy lived in great houses filled with the best possessions from all over the world.

## The Family

An average family might include a man and wife, their oldest son and his wife, and their other unmarried children. Often a grandparent or other widowed or unmarried relative lived with them. Often two or three houses were built close together, sometimes around a large courtyard, forming a compound that housed an extended family of other married sons and their families.

Within the home, a woman cared for her family, grinding corn, baking, cooking, and waiting on her husband and his guests. Here women spun and wove cloth for their own use and to sell in the market. The women were also the water carriers, drawing water from the fountains and carrying it home in large jugs. In the farming communities, the women also worked in the fields. Young girls learned by helping their mothers, but boys began to study the Scriptures when they were five years old. By the time they were thirteen, most boys had finished their education.

## The Work

The great mass of men were farm workers, shepherds, fishermen, or day workers in the fields, but in the bigger towns they worked at many different trades, including carpenters, dyers, scribes, weavers, tentmakers, potters, and metalsmiths. These crafts were often hereditary, passing from father to son.

Most of the people were poor, and there was almost no middle class. At the local markets and fairs, the people sold their corn, wine, figs, and cloth and bought tools, shoes, jewels, and scents. Traveling merchants and peddlers competed with the shopkeepers in the towns and cities.

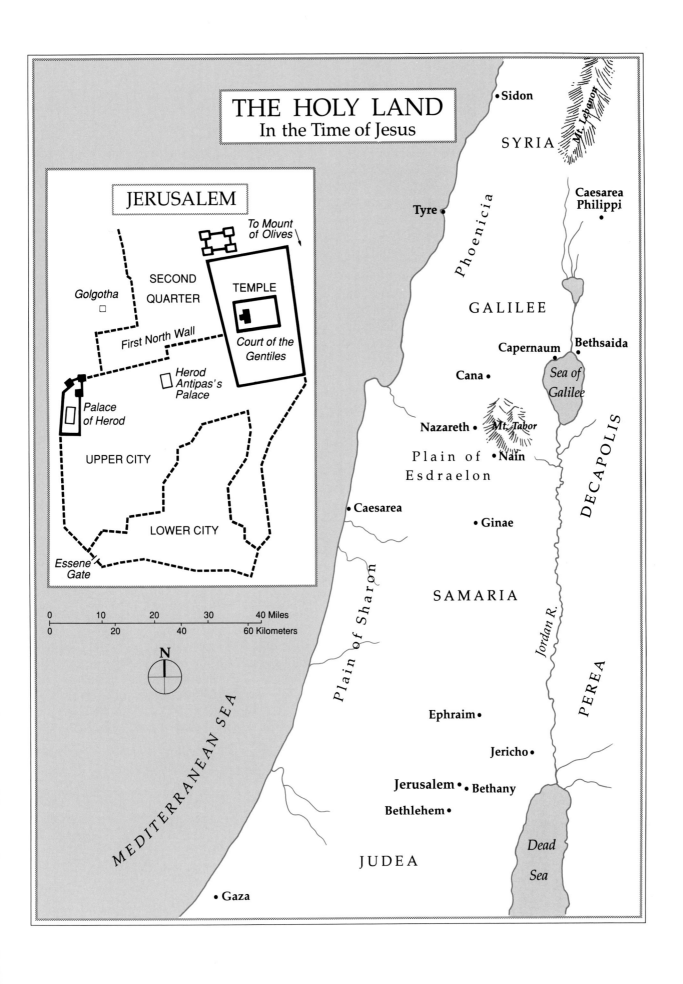

# THE HOLY LAND
## In the Time of Jesus

### JERUSALEM

*To Mount of Olives*

SECOND QUARTER

*Golgotha*

TEMPLE

First North Wall

*Court of the Gentiles*

*Herod Antipas's Palace*

*Palace of Herod*

UPPER CITY

LOWER CITY

*Essene Gate*

0    10    20    30    40 Miles
0    20    40    60 Kilometers

N

• Sidon

SYRIA

*Mt. Lebanon*

Caesarea Philippi

• Tyre

*Phoenicia*

GALILEE

Capernaum • Bethsaida

*Sea of Galilee*

Cana •

Nazareth • *Mt. Tabor*

*Plain of Esdraelon* •Nain

DECAPOLIS

• Caesarea

• Ginae

*Plain of Sharon*

SAMARIA

*Jordan R.*

PEREA

Ephraim •

MEDITERRANEAN SEA

Jericho •

Jerusalem • • Bethany

Bethlehem •

Dead Sea

JUDEA

• Gaza

# RELIGION IN THE TIME OF JESUS

Jesus was born into the Jewish religion, and his words often refer to Jewish law or tradition. However, in his time there were several different religious groups within the Jewish community, and they did not agree on the correct way to practice the religion.

## The Pharisees

The Pharisees were a group that followed strict religious laws and kept apart from unbelievers and from other Jews. They have been traced to the Hasidim, or "holy ones," who arose in the 4th or 5th century B.C. and stressed the study of the Torah (the first five books of the Old Testament). By the time of Jesus, the doctrines of the Pharisees represented the religious beliefs and practices of a large part of the Jewish community.

The Pharisees believed that the law given to Moses consisted of the written law, or Pentateuch, and the oral law, or unwritten religious tradition. They insisted that religion must continue to grow, and they interpreted the teachings of Judaism for the common people. The Pharisees believed that God was not satisfied by bloody sacrifices, and that religious observance did not depend solely on the Temple and its ritual.

Many doctrines of the Pharisees were similar to later Christian belief. The Pharisees believed in angels, in the resurrection of the dead, and in immortality. Their doctrines prepared the ground for belief in a Messiah.

The Pharisees are generally described in the Bible as paying too much attention to the fine details of religious law and not enough attention to the true spirit of religion.

## The Sadducees

The Sadducees were a religious group that arose after the Maccabean revolt of the 2nd century B.C. They traced their group back to Zadok, who was appointed by King Solomon as chief priest of the Temple in Jerusalem. Their influence grew during the Roman occupation and remained strong until the fall of Jerusalem in 70 A.D.

Representing mainly the conservative, priestly tradition in Judaism, the Sadducees accepted only the written Mosaic law and refused to recognize the oral law (the Talmud) as binding. They did not believe in immortality, believing that the soul died with the body.

The Sadducees were worldly people who came from wealthy, more aristocratic elements of Jewish society than did the Pharisees, who tended to be more identified with the common people. The Sadducees cooperated willingly with the political rulers and held considerable power over the life of Jews in Palestine. Because they depended on the rituals of the Temple, their influence declined considerably after the Temple was destroyed.

## The Essenes

The Essenes were a sect of about 4,000 members, living in Palestine from about 100 B.C. to 100 A.D. The Essenes are not mentioned in the New Testament, but other ancient documents describe them as following a life of withdrawal and community sharing.

Sometime in the late 2nd century B.C., the Essenes set up headquarters along the western side of the Dead Sea. The famous Dead Sea Scrolls may have belonged to the Essenes. Evidence indicates that the members of the community slept in caves or huts, prayed, studied, and ate in communal buildings, and owned property communally.

The Essenes had their own interpretation of the law and their own religious calendar. They believed that all prophecy would come true in their time and that they would fight in the great final battle between good and evil.

## The Zealots

The Zealots were a group of fanatically brave and reckless men who rose against the Romans. Their attitude toward the law probably differed little from that of the Pharisees, but they were not willing to keep the law and wait. They preferred to strike for independence against all odds, trusting that God would come to their aid.

# THE WORK OF THE APOSTLES

When the Apostles returned to Jerusalem after the Ascension of Jesus, they continued to meet and pray with the believers, a group of about 120 people. Matthias was chosen by lot to replace Judas as the twelfth Apostle.

## Pentecost

On the day of Pentecost, the twelve Apostles were together when they were filled with the Holy Spirit. Tongues of fire rested upon them, and they began to speak in the languages of all nations. A number of people gathered, drawn from the crowd of Jews in Jerusalem for the feast. They thought the apostles were drunk with wine. Peter explained that they were not drunk, but filled with the Holy Spirit. He warned the people to repent and be baptized in the name of Jesus for the forgiveness of their sins. Three thousand people were baptized that day and joined the group of believers.

## Converts and Dissension

The group ate together and held their property in common, living communally as Jesus had taught them. As they went each day as one family to pray in the Temple, others saw them and joined them. One day, at the Temple gate, a crippled beggar asked them for money. Peter told him to stand and walk in the name of Jesus Christ of Nazareth, and helped him to stand. The beggar went into the Temple with them, leaping and praising God. As word of this spread through the city, more and more people joined the group.

The teaching of the Apostles disturbed the priests of the Temple and the elders, particularly the Sadducees, who did not believe in resurrection. The Jewish authorities objected to the claim that Jesus was the Messiah and that belief in him would bring forgiveness of a person's sins. Peter and John were arrested as they were speaking to the people. But they boldly defended their faith before the authorities, who found nothing to say in opposition and released them with a warning to speak no more in the name of Jesus.

## Stephen, The First Christian Martyr

The Hebrew-speaking Jews looked down on Greek-speaking Jews who had come to Jerusalem. The Greeks complained that the widows of their group were overlooked in the daily distribution of food. The Apostles told the people to choose seven wise, good men from among themselves to handle such problems. Stephen was one of those chosen.

Some members of the synagogue disputed with Stephen, and they instigated others to claim that he had spoken against Moses and God. In defending himself, Stephen argued that Solomon was wrong to build the Temple because God does not live in a house made by human hands He called the Jews traitors and murderers, accusing them of treating Jesus as they had treated all God's messengers. The angry crowd drove him from the city and stoned him to death.

## Two Visions

The Jews had always believed that they were God's chosen people. The first Christians, and of course Jesus and his twelve disciples, were all Jews. It was not until the disciples began to spread the Gospel throughout the world that Gentiles (non-Jews) became a part of the church.

Cornelius, a Roman centurion in Caesarea, was a Gentile who believed in and prayed to God. He had a vision in which an angel appeared and told him to send messengers to bring the apostle Peter to Caesarea.

As Peter was praying on the rooftop the next day, he fell into a trance and he had a strange vision. He saw heaven open and a vessel come down, shaped like a great sheet tied at all four corners and filled with all kinds of animals, birds, and reptiles. A voice commanded, "Rise, Peter; kill, and eat."

Peter, as a Jew, was prohibited from eating certain kinds of flesh, and so he replied, "No, Lord, for I have never eaten anything that is common or unclean." Twice more the voice repeated the command, and then the vessel rose again into heaven.

As Peter puzzled over this dream, the messengers arrived and called for him. The Spirit spoke to Peter, saying, "Behold, three men seek you, Rise and go with them, doubting nothing, for I have sent them."

Peter went with the men and found Cornelius and a gathering of people waiting for him. Peter then understood his dream and said to the people, "You know that it is unlawful for a Jew to keep company with one of another nation. But God has showed me that I should not call any man common or unclean." Then Peter preached the Gospel to the Gentiles and baptized them.

## Conflict within the Church

Many Christian Jews were not pleased about allowing Gentiles into the church. The Jews had shunned all but the most unavoidable contact with non-Jews. Gentiles ate animals and parts of animals that the Jews were forbidden to eat. Gentiles were not circumcised, and only those circumcised in accordance with the law of Moses were considered God's people.

Some Jewish Christians argued that Gentiles who were not circumcised could not be saved. Others replied that Gentiles did not have to follow the laws of Moses to be included in the new church. Finally, a council was called in Jerusalem at which the Apostles and elders of the church debated these issues. The council decided that Gentile converts did not have to be circumcised, but that they would have to follow some of the laws of Moses, such as not eating sacrificial meat.

## On the Road to Damascus

A man named Saul had approved of the stoning to death of Stephen, and he had become known as the harshest and most feared persecutor of Christians following this stoning. Saul was so dedicated to hunting down and capturing Christians that he obtained letters from the high priest in Jerusalem to the synagogues in Damascus. The letters gave him the authority to arrest anyone in Damascus who spoke of a belief in Jesus.

On Saul's journey to Damascus, a great light from heaven shone around him. Saul fell to the ground and he heard a voice saying,

"Saul, Saul, why do you persecute me."

Saul asked, "Who are you, Lord?"

And the voice said, "I am Jesus, whom you are persecuting."

Trembling, Saul asked, "Lord, what will you have me do?"

And the Lord said to him, "Get up, and go into the city, and you shall be told what you must do."

The men with Saul stood speechless, hearing a voice, but seeing no one. Saul arose, but when he opened his eyes, he could not see. The men led him to Damascus.

Three days later, the Lord sent one of the disciples, Ananias, to give Saul his sight back. Ananias was afraid, for he knew of Saul's reputation as a cruel persecutor of the Christians. But he went to Saul and laid his hands on him and Saul regained his sight.

Saul spent some time among the Christians in Damascus. Then he began going into the synagogues—where he had once intended to arrest Christians—and began to preach in the name of Jesus. Saul later changed his name to Paul and dedicated the rest of his life to spreading the Gospel to the Gentile world.

## Paul: Missionary to the Gentiles

The founding of the congregation in the Roman colony of Antioch is typical of the way the Gospel was introduced to new lands. After arriving in Antioch, Paul and Barnabas went to the synagogue on the sabbath day. After the reading of the law and the prophets was finished, the elders of the synagogue asked if the strangers would like to speak.

Paul stood up and began by recounting the history of the Israelites, a story his listeners knew well. He then reminded them of God's promise to send Israel a Savior, and gave evidence of the ways in which Jesus fulfilled the prophesies, thus proving that Jesus was the long-awaited Savior.

Many of the Jews believed what Paul had told them and became converts. As they left the synagogue, the people asked Paul and Barnabas to speak again on the next sabbath. That day a great crowd of Jews and Gentiles gathered to hear them preach. They made many new converts, both Jew and Gentile, but they also encountered opposition.

The Jewish authorities stirred up the people in Antioch against Paul and Barnabas, and drove them from the city. This was often the case, but although the Apostles themselves were driven from a town, they left behind a core group of believers—a new church.

## Paul's Accomplishments

Paul was an energetic man. He turned to spreading Christianity with the same force and effort he had once applied to persecuting the Christians. Paul made three missionary journeys, each lasting some years. Everywhere he went he started new churches. And everywhere he went he encountered opposition. He was stoned, whipped, jailed, and driven from cities many times, but his belief in the value of his mission never wavered.

Paul worried over each new church. Whenever he heard of problems, he wrote letters to the churches, advising, exhorting, and pleading with them to solve their problems.

## The Greatest of These Is Love

Even Paul's favorite church, in Corinth, was not immune to problems. Some of the members began to look down on those who lacked the same gifts. Those who could speak in tongues (foreign or unknown languages), for instance, felt superior to those who could not. Paul wrote to them, "If I speak in the tongues of men and angels but have not love, I am like sounding brass, or a tinkling cymbal. . . . Every other gift dies, save three alone which have no end. . . . Faith and hope and love go on forever, these three; but the greatest of these is love."

## Paul's Imprisonment

Paul's work among the Gentiles had created mistrust in the Jewish community. Therefore, Paul agreed to quiet these suspicions by undergoing purification rites with four Jerusalem Christians. However, some Jewish pilgrims from Asia saw Paul at the Temple and stirred up the crowd by accusing him of taking an unclean Gentile into the forbidden part of the Temple. People came running from all over the city and dragged Paul from the Temple. In the midst of the riot, Roman soldiers appeared and took Paul into protective custody.

Twice Paul tried to defend himself, once speaking to the crowd and once to the Sanhedrin. In his speech to the Sanhedrin, Paul exploited the differences between the Pharisees and the Sadducees on the question of resurrection, once again causing a riot.

After learning of a plot against Paul's life, the Romans sent him to Caesarea. Felix, the governor, heard the case but was unwilling either to acquit Paul or condemn him and left him in prison. Festus, his successor, reopened the case, and Paul, who thought he would be sent to Jerusalem to stand trial, exercised his right as a Roman citizen and appealed to Caesar. After conferring with his advisers, Festus decided to send Paul to Rome.

## Storm and Shipwreck

Paul, together with other prisoners, sailed for Rome in late fall. The ship was caught by winds of hurricane force and driven toward the middle of the Mediterranean Sea. As the storm raged, the cargo was thrown overboard and all hope of being saved was lost. Paul encouraged the others, telling them that an angel had appeared to him and said that the lives of all on board would be saved. On the fourteenth night, they approached land and, just before dawn, the ship ran aground on a sandbar off the island of Malta. The people on board swam or used pieces of the ship to float to shore. After three months on Malta, they again set sail for Rome.

## Paul's Journey to Rome

In Rome, the believers greeted Paul, and the Romans allowed him to live by himself with a soldier as guard. When a Roman citizen appealed to Caesar, there was a two-year period within which his prosecutors had to come to Rome to present their case. Paul, although still under house arrest and in chains, spent the time in his own rented lodgings in Rome, teaching and writing without hindrance. There is no evidence that an appearance before Caesar ever took place.

As word spread and the number of Christian communities grew, more and greater persecutions took place. It is believed that both Peter and Paul died in Rome at some time during the reign of the Emperor Nero.

# THE BIBLE AS A BOOK

The Bible is actually not a single book but many different books collected together in one volume: Genesis, Exodus, Leviticus, and so on. The word *Bible* goes back to a Greek word that means "paper" or "book." The Greek word comes from *Biblios*, which was the Greek name for an important port city on the Mediterranean Sea. From the city of Biblios, the Greeks obtained Egyptian papyrus, a plant material used in the ancient world to make paper for books.

## The Books of the Bible

For Jews, 24 books of the Old Testament make up the Bible. The Christian Bible divides some of these books, so that the Old Testament is made up of 39 different books. The New Testament includes 27 books.

Some Christian Bibles, especially those of Roman Catholic and Eastern Orthodox churches, also include 15 other books of ancient Jewish writing known as the *Apocrypha* ("hidden texts"). In some cases, these books are distributed throughout the Old Testament; in others they are placed separately at the end of the Old Testament.

The first five books of the Old Testament, the Hebrew Torah, are also known as the Five Books of Moses because they include the history and laws of the Israelites up to the time of the death of Moses. Later parts of the Old Testament continue the story of the Israelites and record the work of their great poets, prophets, philosophers, and kings.

The teachings of Jesus are written in the Gospels. The Gospels of Mark, Matthew, and Luke are often called the *Synoptic* ("seen together") Gospels, because they all describe the same events in essentially the same way. The Gospel of John is distinct from the others, using different episodes and a different sequence of events to tell the story of Jesus.

The books of the Bible contain nearly every type of writing including historical narratives, prayers, proverbs, prophecies, poetry, songs, parables, legal codes, letters, and instruction in religious rituals and daily affairs.

## Translations of the Bible

The first written form of the Bible was of course not in English; the English language did not even come into existence until about 400 to 500 years after the birth of Christ.

The Old Testament first appeared in the Hebrew language, and the New Testament first appeared in an ancient form of Greek. From early times, however, believers wanted to share the Bible's teachings with people who could not understand Hebrew or Greek. In order to spread the Word of God, they had to translate the Bible into other languages.

In many parts of the Holy Land, the Jewish people spoke a language called Aramaic, which was closely related to Hebrew but distinct from it. Jesus and his disciples spoke a form of Aramaic. In Aramaic-speaking communities, a preacher would read the Bible in Hebrew, and a translator standing nearby would repeat the words in Aramaic. These versions were called *Targum*, a Hebrew word meaning "translation."

About the year 250 B.C., Jewish scholars in Alexandria, Egypt, translated the entire Old Testament into Greek, which had become the language of culture after the conquests of Alexander the Great. This Greek translation is called the *Septuagint* ("seventy") because seventy people were said to have worked on it. Many of the early Christians spoke Greek, so they could understand the Septuagint.

## The Latin Bible

As Christianity spread throughout the world, translations were made into other languages. A Latin translation appeared in the second century A.D. Around 400 A.D., Eusebius Hieronymus, a scholar we now know as St. Jerome, revised the Latin Bible. His version became known as the *Vulgate*, because it was written in what was then known as "vulgar" language, meaning the ordinary language of the common people. For centuries, the Vulgate was the only Bible authorized by the Roman Catholic Church, and

Latin became the means by which the Word was spread throughout the Western world. In the Eastern Christian churches, the Greek Bible remained the standard text.

## Bibles for the Common People

Throughout the Middle Ages, the Bible was unavailable to most people. Copies of the Bible had to be made by hand and were rare and expensive. And since Bibles were written in Latin and Greek, few people other than scholars and clergy could read them. In the 15th and 16th centuries, though, all this was changed by two major historical developments: the invention of the printing press and the Protestant Reformation.

About the year 1450, Johannes Gutenberg invented the type mold, which made possible the printing of books from movable type. With the development of printing, hundreds of copies of a book could be made for the cost of a single hand-printed volume. For the first time, the Bible was available in the form of multiple, relatively inexpensive copies.

In the early 1500s, dissent in the Catholic Church led to the rise of Protestant religions. The fact that the Bible was then available only in Latin was a major issue in the Protestant Reformation. In 1521, Martin Luther translated the Bible into German so that the common people could read it themselves.

## The Bible in English

Soon after Martin Luther's German Bible appeared, William Tyndale began the first translation of the Scriptures from the original Hebrew and Greek into English. In order to avoid arrest in England, where only the Latin Bible was permitted, Tyndale fled to Europe. There he published his English translations of the New Testament (1526) and the Five Books of Moses (1530) before being arrested and executed in 1536 as a heretic (someone who opposes or rejects an official religious belief). His dying words were, "Lord, open the King of England's eyes." By the following year, Tyndale's prayer had been answered: King Henry VIII of England broke with the Catholic Church, established the Church of England, and sanctioned an English Bible based on Tyndale's work.

## The King James Bible

In the year 1604, King James I of England appointed a group of scholars to produce a new, more accurate translation of the Bible in his name. Published in 1611, the King James Version was hailed as a masterpiece of English literature, and it became the standard Bible for most English-speaking churches.

Over the years, though, some words of the King James Version have come to sound old-fashioned to English speakers. The English language has changed since the King James Version was published. For example, *thou, thy,* and *thine* then were common words, but they have largely passed out of use and been replaced by *you, your,* and *yours.*

Also, people's knowledge of the original Scriptures has changed. Archaeologists in the Middle East have unearthed hundreds of ancient manuscripts, including both commentaries on Biblical texts and copies of the texts themselves. By comparing these manuscripts, Biblical scholars have gradually derived a more accurate text. At the same time, studies of other texts have improved knowledge of ancient Greek and Hebrew, allowing translators to come closer to the original meaning.

## Recent Bibles

In both England and the United States, groups of religious scholars have made efforts to revise and update the King James Version. In 1870, the Church of England authorized a revision that corrected some errors in the King James, but it was widely seen as "too literal" and it did not replace the King James in either church or private use.

The Revised Standard Version, published in 1946–57, set out to preserve the poetry of the King James as much as possible but to update it wherever its meaning had become unclear. According to its editors, the meanings of more than 300 words in the Bible had significantly changed in the three centuries since the King James was published.

Recent notable translations of the Bible include *The New English Bible* (1961–70), *The Jerusalem Bible* (1966), *The New American Bible* (1970), *The Good News Bible* (1976), and *The New International Version* (1978).

# NOTES ON THE TEXT

**The Creation, Pages 1–4:** Light was God's first creation following the initial creation of the heaven and the earth. "And God said, 'Let there be light.'" Throughout the Bible, light is associated with God and with life.

The term "man," which occurs frequently in the Creation and elsewhere in the text, is a rendering of the Hebrew word *Adam*, which has been translated as *man* in the collective sense of "human being" rather than in the specific sense of "a male person."

The break in the Creation account between the end of Genesis 1 and the beginning of Genesis 2 is a reflection of the fact that the early Bible was not divided into chapters. Formal chapter divisions were added later, in the Middle Ages, and they do not always reflect a significant change in subject matter.

**The Garden of Eden, Pages 6–7:** The location of the Garden of Eden has never been determined, but both Egypt and Mesopotamia have been considered to be possibilities. The name *Eden* means "delight" or "pleasure" in Hebrew. This has been traced to a Sumerian word that means "plain." Sumer was one of the earliest civilizations in the Mesopotamian plain, watered by the Tigris and Euphrates Rivers. The soil of this area was extremely fertile and has been under cultivation for thousands of years.

**The Forbidden Fruit, Pages 8–10:** The fruit that Adam and Eve eat in the Garden of Eden has traditionally been pictured as an apple. Actually, the Bible does not mention a specific kind of fruit, saying only that "when the woman saw that the tree was good for food, and that it was beautiful, and that it was a tree to make one wise, she took its fruit, and she did eat."

**Cain and Abel, Pages 11–12:** God banished Cain for murdering his brother and set a mark upon him. The "mark of Cain" has come to be associated with a murderer. But the mark is to protect Cain, "so that anyone finding him would not kill him." His punishment comes from God.

**The Lord Speaks to Noah, Page 13:** The statements given here and elsewhere divide the animal kingdom into four groups: man, beast, creeping things, and the birds of the air.

Many ancient peoples thought of living things as falling into four categories: those that walk the earth on two legs (humans); those that walk on four legs (animals); those that go along the earth or in the water (snakes, fish, insects); those that fly above the earth (birds).

**Noah and the Ark, Pages 14–17:** Noah sends forth a dove from the ark to see if the waters had dried up from the earth. The dove eats only plants, so if it finds food, Noah will know the waters have receded. The dove returns with an olive leaf in her mouth. Knowing that olive trees grow at a low elevation, Noah has the sign that "the waters had gone down from off the earth."

The universal use of a dove with an olive branch as a symbol of peace can be traced to this account.

**Noah Hears God's Promise, Page 18:** A rainbow appears when the sun emerges after a storm, an indication that the storm is over. After the flood that God sent to punish the wickedness of humanity, he sets a rainbow in a cloud as a sign of his covenant with all living things that "the waters shall no more become a flood to destroy all flesh."

**The Tower of Babel, Page 19:** The city in which the people tried to build a tower to heaven was known as Babel, a word that itself sounds like meaningless talk. The word, which is Assyrian, means "gate of God," but it is very close to the Hebrew word, *balal,* which means "to confuse."

**Abraham, Pages 20–21:** Abraham is considered to be the founder of the Hebrew people. Two groups that are currently in conflict in the Middle East regard him as a common ancestor: the Jews are descended from him through his son Isaac, and the Arabs are descended from him through Ishmael, his son by Hagar, the servant of Sarah.

**Abraham and Sarah, Page 22:** Though Abraham had been promised the land of Canaan by the Lord, he is now very old. Up to this point, he has no children to whom he can pass on the promised land.

**Sodom and Gomorrah, Page 23:** The lost cities of Sodom and Gomorrah were on the Jordanian Plain near the Dead Sea. The term *sodomy* derives from the idea that the people of Sodom were sexually depraved. The Lord destroyed the cities because he could not find even ten innocent men within them.

**The Test for Abraham, Page 24:** The Bible often refers to sacrifices being offered to God as a form of worship or respect, or to atone for sins. The thing sacrificed had to be valuable, and thus was usually in the form of food, typically cereal grains such as wheat, or an animal, such as a sheep or calf. In the case of animal sacrifice, the term "burnt offering" means the animal was burned on a fire.

**Isaac and Rebekah, Pages 26–27:** Although most marriages were negotiated by the parents, the final arrangements required the consent of the prospective bride. Although Rebekah's father and brother have agreed to give her in marriage to Isaac, Rebekah's consent is also needed.

It was a gesture of respect for both men and women to dismount at the approach of a person of importance, and for a woman to appear veiled. When Rebekah sees a man approaching, she gets down from the camel. And when the servant tells her that it is his master, Rebekah covers her face with her veil. (It is not necessary for her to be veiled before the servant.)

**Jacob and Esau, Pages 28–30:** It was the right of the firstborn, at his father's death, to become the head of the family and receive the largest share of the property, which in Deuteronomy is fixed as a "double portion." Jacob's superiority over Esau, which symbolizes the superiority of Israel over Edom, is thought to have been brought about because of Esau's willingness to give up his birthright to Jacob merely in return for food.

The blessing that Jacob receives by deceiving Isaac is God's blessing, which brings with it good fortune for the person receiving it and all associated with him. In this case, even Laban prospers under Jacob's blessing.

**Rachel and Leah, Pages 32–33:** Leah is brought to Jacob heavily veiled, probably with a long mantle with which her whole body could be wrapped. In the dark, after the celebration of the wedding feast, it is not unlikely that Jacob could mistake Leah for Rachel. This deception by Laban may be regarded as divine retribution for Jacob's deception of his father.

At this time it was possible for a man to marry one woman and then later to marry her sister, as Jacob does with Leah and Rachel. However, after the giving of the Law at Sinai, the marrying of two sisters was forbidden.

**Jacob and the Angel, Page 35:** The Jewish custom of not eating the "sinew of the hip" stems from the strained thigh that Jacob receives here as he wrestles with the angel. The angel then gives Jacob the name "Israel," which in this sense means "he who perseveres with God."

**The Coat of Many Colors, Pages 36–39:** Joseph's coat was probably a long robe with full, wide sleeves, which differed from the knee-length sleeveless tunic most people ordinarily wore. Often tribal chiefs wore such robes woven in many colors as a symbol of their rulership. In giving Joseph such a coat, Jacob marked him as the leader of the tribes after Jacob's death.

**Pharaoh's Dreams, Pages 40–41:** Isolated as a prisoner in a foreign land, Joseph is still able to win a special place in the court of the ruler by his ability to interpret dreams. Many years later in another country, Daniel is able to do the same thing in the court of King Nebuchadnezzar and his son King Belshazzar (pages 140–145).

**Joseph and His Brothers, Pages 42–43:** During the famine, Joseph's brothers "came and bowed down to him with their faces to the ground." Although they were unaware of this, they were fulfilling the prediction of Joseph's dream of the bundles of grain (page 36).

**Benjamin in Egypt, Pages 44–45:** Joseph is described here as weeping on three different occasions: first as he sees his brother Benjamin, then when he reveals to his brothers who he really is, and finally when he is reunited with his father.

**The Birth of Moses, Pages 46–47:** God's striking down of the firstborn of both man and beasts in the land of Egypt (Exodus 11:5) can be seen as a just retribution for the Pharaoh's order to slay all the male babies of the Israelites.

**Moses, Pages 48–51:** Since Moses went on to speak many times as the leader of his people, it is ironic that here he resists this role and is provided with a spokesman, his brother Aaron.

**Pharaoh and the Israelites, Pages 52–53:** In Egypt, bricks were used for paving as well as for buildings. Chopped straw and refuse were mixed with the clay in order to increase its consistency. Archaeologists have excavated some bricks in Egypt made with good straw, some with roots and bits of straw, and some with no straw at all.

**The Plagues of Egypt, Pages 54–55:** Pharaoh is impressed with the power of God only when a crisis exists and he needs help. Each time a plague comes upon the Egyptians, he promises to let the Israelites go if the Lord will stop the plague. But once the plague has been lifted, he always goes back on his promise.

**Passover, Pages 56–57:** The lamb was the most common offering in Jewish sacrifices, both to offer thanks and to remove sin. When Abraham is about to sacrifice his son, God provides a ram to replace Isaac. In the New Testament, John the Baptist refers to Jesus as the "Lamb of God, who takes away the sins of the world."

**The Parting of the Sea, Page 58:** The Hebrew name for the sea that the Israelites crossed is "the Sea of Reeds" or "Reed Sea." It is in the Greek version of the Old Testament that it is first called "the Red Sea." Its exact location is not known, but it may be the northern part of the present Red Sea.

**In the Wilderness, Pages 60–61:** Large flocks of quail still migrate across the Sinai Peninsula between Arabia and Europe. Often these birds can be captured when, exhausted by their long flight, they roost on the ground or in low bushes.

**The Ten Commandments, Pages 62–64:** In the Sixth Commandment, the word "kill" is also translated as "murder."

**The Tabernacle, Page 65:** Pure olive oil was used for all sacred purposes. The olives were gently pounded in a mortar, and the first drops were considered to be of the purest quality. Because no sunlight fell into the sanctuary, the lamp had to be kept burning at all times.

**The Golden Calf, Pages 66–68:** The Hebrew word actually refers to a "young bull" rather than a calf. The bull was a common religious symbol to the Egyptians and among many Semitic tribes, representing energy and strength. In recent years archaeologists have found such idols in the Middle East.

**The Journey to Canaan, Pages 71–72:** The number forty has special significance in the Bible. Here the Israelites explore the land for forty days, and the Lord then condemns them to wander in the desert for forty years, one year for each of these days. The Great Flood remains on the earth for forty days; Moses spends forty days on the mountain; and Jesus fasts in the wilderness for forty days. The time during which Jesus was seen on earth after his resurrection was forty days.

**The Death of Moses, Page 73:** Moses led the Israelites out of slavery, and God showed him the promised land of Canaan from a mountain. But Moses did not go into the land; he died first.

**The Walls of Jericho, Pages 74–75:** At the beginning of the Israelites' flight from Egypt, God parted the waters of the sea to allow them to cross safely. Here in a similar incident, the waters of the Jordan River dry up and the Israelites cross on dry ground into the Promised Land.

**Gideon's Trumpet, Pages 76–77:** The trumpet or horn of the Old Testament was not a musical instrument, but was used to make a loud sound. It was usually made of the curved horn of a cow or ram, and was used primarily to give signals in war or to announce important events. The horn, called a *shofar,* is still used by Jews at solemn festivals.

**Samson, Pages 79–82:** The Nazirites were a group devoted to the Lord by a special vow. According to this vow, it was forbidden for them to drink alcohol, to cut their hair, to touch or go near a dead body, or to eat unclean food. This vow was originally a lifelong obligation, and it was considered a sin against God to tempt a Nazirite to break it.

**Ruth and Naomi, Pages 84–86:** When Boaz orders his men to leave some grain in the field for Ruth, he is following a law from Leviticus, which states that the corners of the field should not be harvested and grain that falls to the ground should not be gathered but should be left "for the poor and the strangers." Boaz goes even further by telling the men to "let some fall on purpose."

**Samuel Is Called, Pages 87–88:** It was believed that God is responsible for a woman's ability to have a successful pregnancy and bear a child. Thus a woman who was barren (unable to have children) would be regarded as one who is without divine approval, and the woman so affected felt disgrace in the eyes of the world. Sarah, Hannah, and Elizabeth were all barren until they were very old, when God granted them sons.

**Saul and Samuel, Pages 89–91:** The Amalekites roamed the region from the boundary of Judah to the Sinai peninsula and were probably people the Israelites found already in the land. During the Exodus from Egypt, the Amalekites harassed the Israelites and fought to prevent them from entering the region. The Lord then had Moses write that "I will utterly blot out the remembrance of Amalek from under heaven." (Exodus 17:14)

**The Shepherd Boy, Pages 92–93:** The position of armor-bearer was held by a young man who carried the shield, breastplate, a supply of darts, and other weapons for his chief. He also delivered the death blow to those his chief struck down.

**David and Goliath, Pages 94–96:** Goliath is a giant, descended from the giants, mentioned in Genesis, who were said to have been on the earth. Modern archaeologists have found human skeletons of about the same height as Goliath.

**Saul's Jealousy, Pages 98–99:** Saul's periods of black melancholy and flashes of homicidal violence were attributed to an evil spirit from God; today he might be diagnosed as having a form of mental illness.

**David and Jonathan, Pages 100–101:** Jonathan goes to eat with his father Saul at the time of the new moon. The moon, along with the sun, was considered a fertilizing power, as well as a source of light. The appearance of the new moon was an occasion for celebration, often including the blowing of trumpets and an offering of sacrifices.

**The Witch of Endor, Pages 102–103:** A spirit, usually an underground spirit, was thought to be able to dwell in a human being. Such spirits were supposed to have the power of calling up and consulting the dead. Saul goes to consult the witch even though his own policy forbids this.

**David Becomes King, Pages 104–105:** The high places that David mentions were his mountain strongholds, not the high places of worship.

**David and Bathsheba, Pages 106–107:** The Hittites were an ancient people who had settled in the country in earlier times. The few who still remained in the time of David joined with the Israelites, taking Hebrew names, such as Uriah.

What David did was wrong, even though he was the king. It is clear that David is aware of this, for when the prophet Nathan rebukes him, David replies, "I have sinned against the Lord."

**David and Absalom, Pages 108–109:** David's leniency with his sons had a strong impact on the affairs of Israel. Amnon was not punished by David for the rape of his sister, Tamar, though he should have been exiled. Absalom was allowed to return from exile, without being punished for the murder of his brother. The deaths of Amnon and Absalom moved Solomon closer to becoming king, though he was originally far down the line of succession.

**The Death of David, Page 110:** It was not a strict practice that the oldest son became king on the death of his father. Thus there is no objection when Solomon ascends to the throne in place of Adonijah, the eldest of David's remaining sons.

**Solomon's Dream, Page 111:** This dream has been linked to the practice of sleeping in a sacred place in order to receive a communication from the Lord during sleep, since Gibeon was a great high place to which Solomon went to offer sacrifice. There is no indication, however, that he was intentionally seeking this communication. In fact, the Lord is pleased that Solomon does not ask for riches and honor, and so grants him these things.

**King Solomon's Wisdom, Pages 112–113:** The true mother would rather see her child go to another woman than have the child be killed. The false mother, whose own child was already dead, was willing to let this child die. King Solomon's decision parallels the Lord's action with respect to Solomon: he received riches and honor from the Lord specifically because he did not ask for them; here the woman who would give up the child is the one who receives it.

**Solomon Builds a Temple, Page 115:** The original Temple of Jerusalem that was built by Solomon was later destroyed by the Babylonians under King Nebuchadnezzar, in about 586 B.C. The Temple was later rebuilt and destroyed several times, most recently by the Romans in 70 A.D. Today only remnants of the Temple of Herod the Great remain standing, most notably the Western (Wailing) Wall in Jerusalem.

**The Queen of Sheba, Pages 116–117:** There were no major military operations in Solomon's reign, but he put himself in a position of strength by establishing a strong standing army. Figures as to the size of the army vary, but he probably had about 1,400 chariots, 4,000 stables for chariot horses, and some 12,000 horses.

**A Divided Kingdom, Pages 118–119:** The many marriages of King Solomon were probably for political reasons, to strengthen ties with foreign powers. However, even though kings and persons of wealth or authority were permitted to have multiple wives, the Biblical accounts of men who did this, such as Solomon, Jacob, and David, seem to illustrate the troubles inherent in this practice.

**The Prophet Elijah, Pages 120–121:** There is evidence that the worship of the god Baal existed in ancient Palestine as early as 1800 B.C. Although many minor local gods bore the name, Baal was specifically the name of the Amorite god of winter rain and storm. Sculptures show him as a warrior-god, carrying a thunderbolt-spear and a mace. His association with fertility was expressed by the bull, whose horns he wore on his helmet.

**The Return to Jerusalem, Page 122:** The foreign rulers of Jerusalem were usually very hostile toward the Jewish religion and Jewish holy places. Two exceptions to this harsh policy were the Persian kings Cyrus the Great and Darius the Great (Darius I). After the Chaldeans (Babylonians) had destroyed Jerusalem in about 586 B.C., Cyrus in turn conquered Babylonia in 538 B.C. His policy of restoring the Jewish state was later continued by Darius, who ruled from 522 to 486 B.C.

**Esther, Pages 124–125:** The name Ahasuerus is a Hebrew version of Xerxes, the Persian name by which this ruler is more often known historically.

**Mordecai and Haman, Pages 126–127:** The saving of the Jews from Haman is still celebrated on the 14th and 15th of the month of Adar (February or March). It is called the Feast of Purim, which means "lots," because of the lot Haman cast to determine the date for the destruction of the Jews.

**Job, Pages 128–131:** The name *Satan* is a Hebrew word. "The Satan" means "the accuser" or "the adversary." In the early passages of the Old Testament, there is no reference to a distinct being called Satan. It is not until the story of Job that Satan appears as a being whose function is to search out human sin. However, even here he does not have the power to act without the permission of God. In the New Testament, the name *Satan* is used to describe a being who acts independently to tempt Jesus and others. Satan is said to enter the disciple Judas as he betrays Jesus.

**Isaiah, Pages 138–139:** The word "virgin" (Isaiah 7:14) is also translated as "young woman," "girl," or "maiden." The Hebrew word is *almah*, the feminine form of *elem*, "young man."

The wolf of ancient Palestine is larger and lighter in color than the wolf of northern Europe. It is rarely seen today and seldom travels in packs, although it is often found in pairs. The wolf was one of the greatest terrors of the shepherd, ravaging the flocks at night. Lions have been extinct in Palestine since the Crusades, but they must have been common there at one time. Their terrifying roar has been compared to the voice of God, and the nation of Israel has been likened to the lion.

**King Nebuchadnezzar, Page 140:** Visions and dreams were believed to reveal the future. People such as Daniel, who could understand and explain these visions and dreams, were highly regarded by kings, who consulted with them before making important decisions about the rule of the kingdom.

**Handwriting on the Wall, Pages 141–143:** The dye used for the color scarlet was derived from the cochineal insect, which attaches itself to leaves and twigs. In Hebrew, it is called "the scarlet worm." Clothing of scarlet was a mark of distinction and prosperity for those wearing it.

**Daniel in the Lion's Den, Pages 144–145:** During the time of the Babylonian exile, Jerusalem assumed great importance in the religious life of the people. It was the place toward which their prayers were offered. So the offense here is not only that Daniel prays in violation of the king's edict, but also that his prayers are directed toward Jerusalem.

**Jonah and the Whale, Pages 146–149:** The fish that swallowed Jonah has traditionally been considered to be a whale, in spite of the phrase "a great fish." Scientifically speaking, a whale is a mammal rather than a fish, but in earlier times whales were described as "great fish." The distinction between fish and sea mammals is a modern conception.

Jesus identified himself with Jonah, and the experience of Jonah and the whale foreshadows what will happen to Jesus in the tomb. Jesus said, "For just as Jonah was three days and three nights in the whale's belly, so shall the Son of man be three days and three nights in the heart of the earth." (Matthew 12:40)

**The Coming of the Word, Page 153:** John's opening description of Jesus in the New Testament ("In the beginning was the Word") is very similar to the opening of the Old Testament ("In the beginning God created the heaven and the earth.") In the Book of Genesis, the first words of God at the Creation are "Let there be light." John refers to this when he identifies God as "the light."

**Zacharias and Elizabeth, Page 154:** The experience of Zacharias and Elizabeth is comparable to that of Abraham and Sarah. In both cases, the husband and wife are very old, far beyond the usual childbearing age. In both cases, disbelief is shown at first: Sarah laughs when she hears the Lord say that she will have a child, and Zacharias doubts the words of the angel Gabriel.

**The Angel Comes to Mary, Page 156:** Much like Zacharias, Mary is at first fearful, then doubtful when the angel Gabriel appears to her. But unlike Zacharias, Mary then finds favor with the angel. She accepts what he says and declares, "Let me be a servant to the Lord."

**Mary and Elizabeth, Page 157:** The Bible does not give Mary's age at this point in her life. Perhaps because she is the cousin of Elizabeth, who is past childbearing age, Mary has historically been depicted in religious art as a mature woman. However, cousins are often a generation apart in age, and marriage came early in Mary's day. Based on the Hebrew custom of the time, when the marriage took place Joseph would probably have been no more than twenty, and Mary even younger.

**The Birth of John, Page 158:** The name John is translated to mean "the Lord is gracious."

**Joseph and the Angel, Page 159:** Today engagement and marriage are two distinct things. In the time of Jesus, however, the rights and obligations of engagement were nearly identical to those of marriage. Thus Joseph, when he found out that Mary was pregnant, could have subjected her to humiliation by a publicly announced divorce.

**The Birth of Jesus, Page 160:** During the time of Jesus, the people of Judea had to pay a poll tax (personal or "head tax") to the Roman rulers. This was the tax that Joseph and Mary traveled to Bethlehem to pay. In order for this poll tax to be collected by the Romans, they had to take a census of all the people they ruled. Each adult who was enrolled in the census then had to pay a fixed amount of money.

**The Shepherds Come, Pages 162–163:** Jesus is called the Good Shepherd, and he often refers to people as a flock being watched over by a shepherd. Here Jesus himself is visited by actual shepherds from the fields around Bethlehem.

**The Wise Men Visit Jesus, Pages 164–165:** The wise men, or Magi, probably came from Persia. They were men who interpreted human affairs through their study of the stars and through omens and dreams. The traditional belief is that there were three wise men, but the Bible does not say this, though it does mention three gifts that they brought. One Eastern tradition is that there were twelve wise men.

Though the wise men were not Jews, they too were awaiting the birth of the Messiah. The dangerous curiosity of King Herod was aroused by their question, "Where is he that is born King of the Jews?" He considered himself to be the king of the Jews. The Herods were a family who ruled Palestine at the time of Jesus. They were able to maintain power by being friendly with the Romans. When Herod heard of a new king of the Jews, he was suspicious of this possible threat to his rule.

**The Boy in the Temple, Pages 166–167:** Here a young boy brings spiritual wisdom to older men. This incident can be seen as foreshadowing the later message of Jesus that an adult must become like a child to enter the kingdom of heaven.

**John Baptizes Jesus, Pages 168–169:** On several occasions John rejects the idea that he is the Messiah. He speaks a powerful message and has a strong following; in fact at one later point (Luke 11:1), the disciples ask Jesus to teach them to pray as John has taught his followers. But John always makes it clear that he is someone who prepares the way for another, and is not the Messiah himself.

**Jesus Is Tempted, Page 170:** The term "wilderness" usually refers to a place with heavy plant growth. However, in the very dry region of Palestine, a wilderness was any wild, unsettled area away from towns. Rather than having more plant growth than a civilized area, a Biblical wilderness had less, and was more of a desert than a forest.

**Jesus and His Disciples, Pages 172–73:** Jesus takes his first disciples from among fishermen. Fishermen in the time of Jesus supplied one of the main items in the everyday diet. Fish, both dried and salted as well as fresh, were eaten far more often among the ordinary people than was meat.

"Fishers of men" is a play on words, in which the process of spreading the good news of the gospel is compared to fishing, with the "catch" being people's souls rather than fish.

**Jesus Angers the People, Page 174:** This is a demonstration of the old saying that "familiarity breeds contempt." The people of his home town of Nazareth were familiar with Jesus as the son of Joseph, an ordinary carpenter, and so they had a difficult time accepting the idea that he was the fulfillment of the prophecy of Isaiah. Jesus angers the people when he tells them of previous occasions when prophets were sent to help those who were outsiders. Jesus and all his early followers were Jews, and this is is the first indication in Luke that the message of Jesus is for non-Jews as well as for Jews. It is also the first sign that this message will produce hostility within the Jewish community.

**Jesus and Nathanael, Page 175:** Nathanael asks, "Can anything good come out of Nazareth?" He is not saying that Nazareth is an evil place. He is just expressing the idea of that time that it was a small, obscure village that would be unlikely to produce a great leader. Today Nazareth is located in northern Israel and is a city of about 45,000 people, still not very large.

**The Wedding Feast at Cana, Page 176:** Wedding feasts in the time of Jesus were known to last as long as an entire week, so it must have been a common occurrence for the wine to run out at such times.

**A Man Must Be Born Again, Page 177:** Nicodemus comes to Jesus by night because he is a leader of the Pharisees, a group that opposes Jesus, and it would not be politically advisable for him to be seen asking Jesus for guidance. As in many such encounters that Jesus has, Nicodemus does not immediately understand what is said to him. But obviously he goes away and absorbs it, because he later appears at the tomb of Jesus to assist Joseph of Arimathea with the burial, even though that action was very dangerous for him.

**The Living Water, Page 178:** The Samaritans and the Jews were enemies. Both were followers of Moses, but in other ways their beliefs differed. The woman's reference to the patriarch Jacob's having provided the well is part of the conflict of these two groups over which was the true heir to the tradition of their common ancestors.

In the arid land of the Middle East, a well was a very important thing, and a person could even be killed for taking water from a well belonging to some other group. Thus the Samaritan woman finds it very surprising that Jesus, a Jew, would ask her for a drink from a Samaritan well.

**A Dying Child Lives, Page 179:** The story of the officer of the king who begs Jesus to save his dying child has a similarity to the story of Jesus's saving the child of Jairus (page 196). The officer is a high official in the government, while Jairus is a leader of the synagogue. Both men are thus from a higher social class than the fishermen and craftsmen with whom Jesus usually associates.

**Jesus Calls to Simon, Pages 180–181:** The disciple Simon is also known as Peter. The name "Peter" comes from a Greek word that means "rock" or "stone."

**Jesus Heals the Sick, Pages 182–83:** Often when Jesus performs a miraculous act of healing for someone, he warns the person not to make the miracle known to the public. But invariably the event becomes known anyway, and as Jesus's fame grows, so too does the danger that he will be arrested as a threat to the established order.

**A Sick Man Walks Again, Page 184:** This event gives evidence of the large size of the crowds that came to hear Jesus speak, and also shows the great desire of the afflicted people to be healed.

**The Sermon on the Mount, Pages 186–187:** At this point Jesus was already being challenged on the grounds that he and his followers did not correctly obey the laws of Moses. Here he turns the argument around by saying that far from wanting to abolish the laws of Moses, he wants his followers to be even more faithful to the law.

**The Lord's Prayer, Page 189:** The last line of the Lord's Prayer, "For thine is the kingdom, and the power, and the glory, forever. Amen," appears in traditional translations and is therefore presented here. However, many modern scholars regard this passage as something that was added to the Prayer in the early days of the Church rather than as part of the words that Jesus originally taught to his disciples.

Jesus here admonishes the Pharisees for making a public show of prayer, while telling his own followers to shut the door and pray in private.

**The Lilies of the Field, Page 190:** Jesus uses King Solomon as his example of a splendidly clothed ruler. In I Kings 10 there is a detailed description of the great wealth of Solomon's kingdom, and the visiting Queen of Sheba marvels at his prosperity.

**The Golden Rule, Page 191:** This same principle was known to ancient Greek and Jewish philosophers. The Chinese sage Confucius also taught a form of the Golden Rule. Hillel, a Jewish scholar who lived from about 30 B.C. to 10 A.D., said "Whatever is hateful unto thee, do it not unto thy fellow."

**A House Built on a Rock, Page 192:** Here as in many other instances Jesus uses rhythm, repetition, and metaphor in his language to make a point. The concept that his message was originally in spoken, not written, form is conveyed very clearly here.

**Jesus Forgives a Sinner, Page 193:** It has traditionally been assumed that the sinful woman in this episode was a prostitute, though the text does not state this directly. Prostitution is condemned at many points in the Old and New Testaments, though it seems to have continued to exist in spite of this.

**Jesus Calms the Storm, Page 194:** The reference is to the Sea of Galilee, an inland, freshwater body of water that is nearly thirteen miles long and eight miles wide. The Jordan River feeds the lake on the north and runs out of it on the south. Small boats propelled by oars and occasionally sails were used by fishermen on the Sea of Galilee. Because of the great height of the hills surrounding it (up to 2,000 feet in the east), wide temperature changes often occur that can trigger sudden, violent storms.

**Jesus Saves a Child, Page 196:** Jesus allows no one to come with him to the house of Jairus except his disciples Peter, James, and John. These same three later are chosen to accompany Jesus in the Garden of Gethsemane (page 236). This

seems to indicate which of his followers were closest to Jesus.

**Jesus Speaks in Parables, Pages 198–199:** Jesus often presents abstract concepts to his disciples in practical form, using parables. The images are those that would be familiar to the average person of the time, such as fishing, flocks of sheep, farm workers, and plants in the field.

**The Loaves and the Fishes, Pages 200–201:** This episode is one of the very few to be recorded in all four Gospels, and the details are very similar. The Gospels also report that this miracle took place directly after the execution of John the Baptist by King Herod. Thus Jesus obviously has not been driven into hiding by that event.

**Jesus Walks on Water, Page 203:** Peter is often the disciple who is willing to take a bold step forward while the others hang back. Here he is the only one who will attempt to walk on the water. Later, after Jesus is arrested, Peter alone takes the risk of following him to the high priest's palace. Finally, he is the one who is willing to enter the tomb of Jesus, as the other disciple holds back at the entrance.

However, Peter's bold spirit does not always sustain itself. Here his faith wavers and he begins to sink into the water. Later in the high priest's courtyard, he denies three times that he knows Jesus.

**God's Plan for Jesus, Pages 204–205:** The mountain that is associated with this event is Mount Hermon, which is the highest mountain in Syria at about 9,150 feet. The top of this mountain is usually covered with snow all year round.

**Jesus and the Children, Page 206:** The disciples, by scolding the people for bringing their children to Jesus, were reflecting the general attitude of the time that spiritual matters were for adults, not children. For example, in the early years of the custom of baptism, only adults were baptized. It was not until later that baptism of infants become a common practice.

**Jesus Speaks of Forgiveness, Pages 208–209:** This conversation is described by both Luke and Matthew, but only Matthew gives the specific number seventy-seven. Perhaps we can assume that the tax collector Matthew is more precise in his use of figures than is the physician Luke.

**Throwing the First Stone, Pages 210–211:** Stoning a person to death was an ancient method of execution. This is the form of punishment that the accusers of the adulterous woman wanted Jesus to sanction.

This episode is not in some ancient manuscripts and its authenticity is therefore questioned. However, it does display several recurrent themes of the Gospels, such as the effort to test Jesus regarding Mosaic law and his deflecting of the issue rather than making a direct response.

**The Rich Young Man, Page 212:** In many early societies, wealth was regarded as a blessing of the gods, and it was thought that earthly riches would give a person an advantage in the afterlife. Here Jesus opposes this idea by saying that a rich man, rather than having a spiritual advantage, is actually prevented by his wealth from reaching heaven.

**A Blind Man Can See, Page 213:** The Pharisees were one of two main religious groups (the other being the Sadducees) that together made up the Sanhedrin, the religious council ruling over Jewish religious life. The Pharisees were known for their devoted study of Jewish religious law. The teachings of Jesus were generally closer to those of the Pharisees than to other groups. However, on various occasions he depicts them as being more concerned with the appearance of religion than with being truly religious, and more interested in the details of the law than in basic moral principles.

**The Good Samaritan, Page 215:** The Samaritans were enemies of the Jews, and so it is surprising that the Samaritan shows such concern. He even puts himself at risk by accompanying the injured man, since people seeing them together could have assumed that he was the attacker.

The priest may have passed by the injured man because he thought the man was already dead, since religious law stated that a priest should not touch a dead body. This can be seen as an example of the argument by Jesus that certain people followed the fine points of religious law at the expense of basic principles of good conduct.

**Workers in the Vineyard, Pages 216–217:** The workers who had labored all day were jealous when they saw that the workers who had arrived much later were paid the same wage. But the owner did keep his original bargain with the early workers. Also, the later workers did not reject an opportunity to work earlier in the day; they were never asked.

**The Story of the Lost Son, Pages 218–219:** This account of the Prodigal Son is perhaps the most widely analyzed of all the teachings of Jesus, probably because it seems unfair to many people that the son is welcomed back by his father. But Jesus has already prepared his audience for this concept, in the episode of Luke 15:4–7 (also recorded in Matthew 18:10–15) with the Parable of the Lost Sheep. The shepherd takes more joy in finding the one sheep that was lost than in the ninety-nine sheep that were not lost.

**A Man Rises From the Dead, Pages 220–223:** Lazarus rises from his tomb and returns to life, as Jesus himself later does. There was a Jewish belief at this time that the soul lingered near the body after death, but then departed after three days. So after four days Lazarus would have been considered spiritually as well as physically dead.

The shortest verse in the entire Bible is found here: "Jesus wept." (John 11:35)

**Jesus Comes to Bethany, Pages 224–225:** The Roman Empire often allowed its local populations considerable autonomy, as long as there was no unrest. The priests saw that Jesus had a considerable following, and they may have feared he would lead the people into a large-scale uprising against Rome. That would bring harsh repercussions against all Jews and perhaps even cause the loss of the priests' authority.

**Jesus Enters Jerusalem, Pages 226–227:** The triumphant entry into Jerusalem marks one of the few times when Jesus allows people to publicly describe him as the Messiah.

**Jesus Clears the Temple, Page 228:** The chief work of the priests of the Temple was making sacrifices and offerings to God. In the outer courtyard of the Temple there was a large square where vendors sold birds and animals for sacrifice. A thriving business in money-changing existed within the Temple's walls, too. Jews came to the city to pay the annual Temple tax. The Roman money they brought was stamped with the likeness of the emperor. Since Jewish law prohibited images, money-changers were permitted to operate in the square, to change Roman currency to their own currency.

**Things That Are Caesar's, Page 230:** Taxation by the Romans was widely resented by the Jews. The people questioning Jesus probably hoped that he would give the popular answer against paying taxes, since this could have been construed as a call for rebellion against Rome. Instead, Jesus deflects the question.

**Judas Betrays Jesus, Page 231:** The traditional view of Judas is that he is motivated by simple greed. (He is a thief; he wants the thirty pieces of silver.) A more modern view takes into account the political climate of the times. A Messiah was expected who would lead a revolt against the Romans and restore the rule of Israel. When Judas sees that Jesus is not going to take on this role, he betrays him to his Jewish opponents. (The betrayal follows just after the incident in which Jesus resists the opportunity to call on Jews not to pay Roman taxes.)

**The Last Supper, Pages 232–233:** The belief that the number 13 is unlucky is said to come from this incident. The number of people present at this fateful meal is thirteen, Jesus and the twelve disciples.

**Jesus Tells of His Death, Page 234–235:** Here as on earlier occasions in the Gospels, Jesus foretells his fate. But in each case the disciples seem not to grasp the significance of what they are hearing.

**The Garden of Gethsemane, Page 236:** The site of the Garden of Gethsemane is just east of the city of Jerusalem, on the side of the Mount of Olives.

**Jesus Is Captured, Page 239:** The sleeping disciples even at this late point have not grasped the significance of the threat to Jesus.

**Jesus Is Put on Trial, Page 240:** This incident demonstrates the idea that crowds are notoriously easy to manipulate and are fickle in their support. Just seven days before this, large, joyous crowds had welcomed Jesus to Jerusalem. But now the crowd mocks him cruelly and calls for his death.

**Peter Denies Jesus, Page 241:** A major city such as Jerusalem was host to travelers and pilgrims from many areas, and its inhabitants would hear various accents. Jesus and many of his followers were from Galilee, and thus the servant girl's suspicions that Peter was with Jesus were strengthened when she recognized his Galilean accent.

**Jesus Is Brought to Pilate, Page 242:** Pontius Pilate was the Roman governor of Judea at the time of Jesus. Though King Herod had certain royal powers under the Romans, he had no authority to condemn a man to death. Thus Jesus was brought to Pilate, who did have the authority to do this.

**Jesus Is Accused, Page 243:** Other sources of this era have described Pilate as a very harsh ruler. However, he appears here as an ambivalent figure who is hesitant about imposing the death sentence. It may be that Pilate was genuinely affected by the words and demeanor of Jesus, or it may be that he was merely trying to avoid responsibility for this controversial decision.

**Give Us Barabbas, Pages 244–245:** Barabbas had been imprisoned for the same crime that Jesus was charged with, being a revolutionary. He had participated in a rebellion in Jerusalem, and was likely to be crucified for this.

**Jesus Is Condemned, Pages 246–247:** Pilate had secured his post through the influence of Sejanus, a favorite of the Roman emperor Tiberius. Sejanus later fell from power, and this seems to have weakened Pilate's position as governor. On several occasions prior to this incident, Pilate's decisions had been overruled by his superiors. He later was recalled from his post to stand trial for cruelty to his subjects, particularly for an incident in which his troops carried out a massacre in Samaria. According to tradition, he was exiled to Gaul and he committed suicide there.

**Jesus Carries the Cross, Page 248:** It is usually assumed that Jesus carried the entire heavy cross; this would explain the help of Simon of Cyrene. However, the usual Roman method of crucifixion was for the condemned person to carry only the horizontal beam of the cross to the place of execution, where upright posts had already been driven into the ground. It may be that Jesus was too weak from the ordeal preceding the crucifixion to carry the beam alone.

**Jesus Is Crucified, Pages 249–251:** It was the custom in Jerusalem to give the person on the cross a drink of a beverage that was laced with stupefying herbs or alcohol, to help them bear the pain. This is the drink that is offered to Jesus.

**Jesus Is Dead, Page 252:** Crucifixion was not a normal punishment for Roman citizens, but it was commonly used for slaves, foreigners, and hated criminals. Each element of the crucifixion process was meant to present a public display of humiliation and suffering and thus to convey the strongest possible warning to those who might think of rebelling against Roman rule.

**Jesus Is Buried, Page 254:** It was the practice to throw out the bodies of the crucified without proper burial. But the Jews were adamant in their belief that the dead should be buried. Thus it was common for friends of the crucified to obtain the body by purchasing it from the government.

Joseph of Arimathaea was a member of the Sanhedrin, but he was also a devout follower of Jesus, and it is assumed he must have kept his allegiance to Jesus secret during the council's proceedings. After it was all over, however, he risked the council's disapproval by burying Jesus in his own tomb.

**Jesus Has Risen, Page 257:** Joseph's tomb was typical of the wealthier class. Tombs of poorer people were closed off by being walled up, but tombs such as this had a great round stone. The huge stone rested in a groove that ran at a downward slope along the entrance to the tomb. It was held in place with wooden wedges which, when removed, allowed it to roll down into place. Tombs of this type still exist today.

**Jesus Lives Again, Pages 258–259:** Jesus had warned his disciples that they would be persecuted for following him. As is evident from their fright immediately after the crucifixion of Jesus, when they are hiding behind locked doors, they did not have to wait long for the persecutions to begin.

**Jesus Goes Up to Heaven, Page 260:** Jesus told his disciples to be witnesses for him. The apostles were to tell everyone of the life and teachings, the death, and the resurrection of Jesus, which they knew of from firsthand experience.

# BIBLE DICTIONARY

This Bible Dictionary provides a list of words from *The Illustrated Children's Bible*. It explains all the words in this book that could be difficult for a modern reader to understand.

The Dictionary includes three kinds of words. First, it has words from the Bible that are no longer in common use, such as *thou*, which is an older word meaning "you." Second, it has words that are still well-known today, but that have a different meaning in the Bible, such as *company*, which used to mean a large group of people rather than a business. Third, it has words that are still used today on some occasions, but that are not part of our everyday language, such as *decree, forsake,* or *righteous.*

**abomination** a thing that is very bad, wrong, or hateful.

**acacia** a type of tree whose hard wood is used for building.

**adultery** sex between a married man and someone who is not his wife, or between a married woman and someone who is not her husband.

**adversity** a time of trouble or difficulty; a problem that must be overcome.

**almighty** having complete or unlimited power. "Almighty God" means "all-powerful God."

**altar** 1. a raised platform or table where sacrifices or offerings to God or a god are made. 2. a table or stand used as a sacred place in a religious ceremony.

**Amen** a word meaning "That is right" or "Let it be so," often said at the end of a prayer to agree with what has been said.

**angel** a messenger of God; a spiritual being who serves God or is with God.

**anguish** great pain or suffering; deep sorrow.

**anoint** 1. to rub or sprinkle a special kind of oil on a person's body. 2. to do this as a sign that the person has taken on some high office or special position.

**anointest** an older word for *anoints*. "Thou anointest" means "you anoint" (rub with oil).

**apostle** or **Apostle** 1. a name given to the close followers of Jesus who began the early Christian church. 2. especially, a name given to the twelve disciples and Paul.

**ark** the large ship built by Noah to save his family and pairs of every different kind of animal during the great flood.

**ark of the covenant** a special box that was built to hold the two stone tablets on which the Ten Commandments were written.

**armor** a metal coat worn in battle by a soldier to protect his body against enemy weapons.

**armor-bearer** a person who went with a soldier to carry his heavy armor to the battlefield.

**art** an older word for *are*. "Thou art" means "you are."

**asp** a small, highly poisonous snake. The kind mentioned in the Bible is usually identified as the Egyptian cobra.

**ass** a long-eared animal related to the horse, used for riding and for carrying or pulling loads; now more often called a *donkey*.

**astray** away from where it is supposed to be. A sheep that has gone *astray* has wandered off from the rest of the sheep in the flock.

**astrologer** a person who claims to be able to tell what will happen in the future by studying the stars.

**avenge** to have revenge against a person; do something to make up for an earlier wrong or injury. Someone who takes revenge against another person is an **avenger**.

**babe** another word for *baby*.

**balance** or **balances** an instrument that is used for weighing things; the thing to be weighed is placed on one side and balanced by a certain amount of weight on the other side.

**balm** 1. a soft oil or ointment spread on the body as a medicine. 2. anything that helps to ease pain or suffering.

**band** a large group of people. A "band of angels" means "a large number of angels."

**banquet** a large and special meal; a feast.

**baptism** the act or special ceremony of baptizing a person. See BAPTIZE.

**baptize** to place a person in the water, or pour or sprinkle the person with water, as a sign that the person's sins have been washed away and he or she has become pure.

**barley** a type of grain plant similar to wheat, widely grown for food.

**barren** 1. not producing crops or fruit. A *barren* field is one in which no useful plants grow. 2. a word used to describe a woman who cannot have children.

**bear** **1.** to pick something up and take it along; carry a thing. "Bearing gifts" means "Bringing gifts." **2.** to give birth or life to. "To bear a child" means "to have a child." **3.** to have or give. "To bear the blame" means "to have the blame." "To bear false witness" means "to give witness (testify) in a false way."

**bear** a type of large, heavy wild animal; the kind mentioned in the Bible is the Syrian bear.

**beast** any animal, especially a wild animal.

**becometh** an older word for *becomes*.

**begotten** an older word meaning "born." A father's *begotten* son is a son born to him.

**behold** a command or statement meaning, "See this" or "Look, and you will see."

**beloved** very much loved; greatly loved.

**betray** to turn against one's own cause or nation and help the enemy; give a person over to the enemy.

**betrayal** the act of betraying someone.

**betrayer** a person who betrays someone.

**birthright** something that a person has the right to receive because of being born into a certain family; an inheritance. In former times, this often meant that the oldest son in a family would get all or most of the father's land when the father died.

**bless** **1.** to make something holy or sacred. **2.** to be *blessed* means to have the favor of God.

**boils** a disease in which large, painful sores break out on the skin.

**bold** not afraid; having courage; brave.

**bondage** the condition of being held as a slave or prisoner; slavery.

**bore** a past tense form of the verb *bear*. "She bore a son" means "She gave birth to a son."

**borne** a past tense form of the verb *bear*. "She has borne a son" means "She has given birth to a son."

**borrower** a person who borrows something from another.

**bramble** a type of shrub or vine that has sharp thorns.

**bread** **1.** a food made by baking flour or meal from grain. **2.** food in general; any food.

**breathless** out of breath; breathing hard, as from running fast.

**bridegroom** the man at a wedding who is getting married.

**brimstone** an older name for sulfur, a chemical element that catches fire very easily.

**brother** **1.** a man or boy who has the same parents as some other person. **2.** a person who is very close to another in some way, as by being part of the same group.

**bulrush** a type of plant having tall, very thin stems and growing in or near water.

**burden** **1.** a heavy load to carry. **2.** a serious problem or difficulty to deal with.

**burnt offering** see OFFERING.

**bushel** a large basket used to hold fruit, grain, or other food crops.

**butler** a male servant who has charge of the household of a wealthy or powerful person.

**captive** someone who is held prisoner, especially a prisoner in war. To be held in **captivity** means to be held as a prisoner.

**cast** **1.** to throw. To *cast* something away is to throw it away. **2.** to put out. To *cast* a spell is to put a magic spell on someone.

**cast lots** to gamble by throwing (casting) some object or objects (lots) and betting on how the throw will come out. Throwing dice is a form of casting lots.

**cattle** **1.** the common farm animals that produce milk and beef. **2.** farm animals in general; any farm animals.

**cedar** a type of tree having very fine wood, often used in ancient times for temples and other important buildings.

**chamber** a room, especially a bedroom or other private room.

**chamberlain** an officer or high-ranking servant in the household of a king.

**champion** **1.** in modern use, a person or team that wins an important game or contest. **2.** in older use, a man who was the strongest fighter in an army and fought at the head of the army.

**chariot** a small two-wheeled cart pulled by one or more horses, formerly used in warfare.

**chasten** to punish in order to make better; punish in a firm but not cruel way.

**child** **1.** a young person; a son or daughter. **2.** a member of a certain tribe or nation, thought of as a son or daughter of the person who began that group. "The children of Israel" means "all the people of Israel," not just the younger people.

**children** see CHILD.

**clean** **1.** free from dirt; not dirty. **2.** free from a disease, such as leprosy. **3.** acceptable to God. A *clean* beast was an animal that was acceptable to be eaten or to be used for sacrifice.

**cleave** to hold or stick tight; cling.

**cloven** divided into parts. Some animals, such as cattle, deer and sheep, have a *cloven* hoof, meaning that the front of the foot is divided in two.

**cockatrice** a poisonous snake. The cockatrice was supposed to be so deadly that it could kill something just by looking at it.

**coffin** a large box in which a dead body is placed for burial.

**comely** pleasing to look at; pretty or beautiful.

**cometh** an older word for *comes*. "My help cometh" means "my help comes."

**commandment** 1. an order or command that must be obeyed or should be obeyed. 2. one of the Ten Commandments that were given by God to Moses.

**commend** to give something over to another, who will be trusted to take care of it. "Into your hands I commend my spirit" means "I give my spirit over to you."

**company** 1. in modern use, a group of people who operate a business together. 2. in older use, any large group or collection of people or things.

**congregation** a large group of people gathered together, especially a group gathered to worship God.

**contend** to act against some enemy or opposing force; struggle against.

**counsel** advice or guidance given to a person about what to do.

**counselor** a person who guides others as to what to do.

**covenant** a serious and lasting agreement to do or not do a certain thing.

**covet** to want very much to have something that belongs to another person; want to take for one's own.

**craftsman** a man who is skilled in doing work with his hands, as in making things from wood.

**creature** any living being, especially a living thing other than a human.

**crimson** a strong, deep shade of the color red, like the color of blood.

**cross** a large, heavy frame of wood used for crucifixion. See CRUCIFIXION.

**crucify** to put a person to death by means of crucifixion; kill by hanging on a cross.

**crucifixion** 1. a way of executing criminals used in ancient times. Those who were condemned to death by crucifixion were nailed or tied to a cross and left hanging there until they died. 2. **the Crucifixion.** the death of Jesus in this way.

**cubit** an ancient measure of length based on the length of the arm, equal to about 18–22 inches.

**cud** in grass-eating animals such as cattle, a mass of partly-digested food chewed a second time.

**cunning** very smart and skillful; able to do or learn things quickly.

**curse** to wish great harm to a person; call on God or a god to bring evil to someone.

**cursed** under a curse; having had evil or harm come to oneself.

**custody** the fact of guarding or keeping safe; care or protection.

**cymbal** one of a pair of round metal plates that are struck together to make a ringing sound.

**cypress** a tall tree whose wood is often used for building.

**dart** a small arrow used as a weapon, thrown by hand rather than shot from a bow.

**dasheth** an older word meaning "throws down hard."

**debt** 1. an amount of money that one person has borrowed from another person and has to pay the person back. 2. a wrong that one person has done to another.

**debtor** a person who owes a debt to someone.

**deceiver** a person who deceives or tricks another person.

**decree** 1. an important order issued by a king or other ruler. 2. to give such an order.

**deed** an action that a person has done; something that is done.

**defy** to speak out or go against someone in a bold way. Goliath *defied* the army of Israel to send someone out to fight him.

**deliver** 1. to send to a certain place. 2. in older use, to take a person away from some harm or evil; save. Daniel was *delivered* (saved) from the danger he faced in the lions' den.

**demon** an evil god or spirit; a devil.

**den** a place where wild animals live, such as a cave or a hole in the ground.

**denarius** a small silver or gold coin used in the ancient Roman Empire. Two or more of these coins are **denarii.**

**deny** to answer something that has been said by saying that it is not true. A person can deny that something happened, deny that he knows someone, and so on.

**descend** 1. to go or come down. 2. to be born later as a relative of a certain person who lived earlier. A grandchild is *descended* from his or her grandparents.

**descendant** a person who is part of a certain family or group, and who is directly related to those who lived earlier in this family or group.

**despise** to dislike very much; hate.

**destruction** the fact of being destroyed; complete ruin or disaster.

**devil** 1. an evil being that has certain powers that humans do not have. 2. **the Devil.** another name for Satan, the chief evil spirit and the enemy of God.

**disciple** 1. a person who is a close follower of a leader. 2. also, **Disciple.** one of the twelve men who followed Jesus to learn from his teaching.

**dominion** the power to rule over or to control something.

291

**draw** to pull or take something up from a lower place, as in getting water from a river or a well.

**dwell** to live in a certain place.

**elder** 1. older. The *elder* son in a family is the older son. 2. one of the older people in a group or tribe. 3. **elders.** a group of older men who have authority in a tribe or nation, either by ruling themselves or by advising the ruler.

**eldest** oldest. The *eldest* daughter in a family is the oldest daughter.

**ember** a piece of wood in a fire, almost burned away but still glowing with heat.

**embrace** to put the arms tightly around; hug or hold tightly.

**endureth** an older word for *endures.* "It endureth forever" means "It endures (lasts) forever."

**enraged** in a great rage; very angry.

**envy** a feeling of wanting what someone else has or of being jealous of that person.

**everlasting** going on for all time; lasting forever.

**evermore** for all time; forever.

**evil** very bad or wrong; not done in a good or right way.

**exile** the fact of being forced out of one's country to live in another country.

**faint** to feel *faint* is to be weak and sick, as from being very hungry or very tired.

**fair** 1. doing or deciding things in the right way; doing what is right. 2. good-looking; pretty or beautiful.

**faith** 1. a strong belief or trust that something will happen in a certain way, without the need for facts or evidence beforehand to prove this. 2. especially, belief in the power and goodness of God, or belief in Jesus as the Son of God.

**false god** a being or object that is worshipped as a god but that is not the true God of the Bible.

**false witness** see WITNESS.

**fame** the fact of being famous; being well-known to people.

**famine** a time when food is very scarce and people have little or nothing to eat.

**fast** to go for a long time without eating anything, by one's own choice rather than because there is no food to eat.

**father** 1. a male parent. 2. a man who is the ancestor of some family, tribe, or nation, especially the person who began that group.

**fatling** a young calf, pig, or other animal that is fed extra food to make it fatter for eating.

**fatted calf** a young calf that has been fed extra food to make it fatter for eating, as for a special feast.

**feast** 1. a large or special meal with certain kinds of food. 2. a holiday or celebration that includes such a special meal. The **Feast of Unleavened Bread,** or Passover, is held each year to celebrate the time when the Israelites were led out of slavery in Egypt.

**fig** a type of small tree that is widely grown for its sweet fruit.

**firstborn** the oldest child in a family.

**flax** a plant whose fibers are used to make thread for clothing.

**fled** a past tense form of the verb *flee.* "He fled" means "He ran away."

**flee** to go away from some danger; run away.

**flesh** 1. the soft part of the body between the skin and the bones. 2. the body of an animal eaten as food; meat. 3. the physical part of a person; the body as opposed to the spirit or soul. 4. people in general; human beings.

**flock** 1. a group of sheep or other animals moving or kept together. 2. a large group of people, thought of as being led or watched over as a shepherd cares for sheep.

**follower** a person who goes along with another and does what that person says; someone who obeys or believes in another person. Those who acted according to the teachings of Jesus were called his followers.

**forbid** to make a rule or law against something; not allow something to be done. Something that is not allowed is **forbidden.**

**forgive** to accept that another person has done wrong and agree not to punish or hate the person for it.

**forgiveness** the act of forgiving; saying that a person who has done wrong will not be punished for it.

**forsake** to give up something and go away from it; leave behind or abandon.

**forth** out of or away from. To **go forth** means to go out from some place to another place. To **bring forth** something means to bring it out from inside, such as a child that is born from its mother's body, or plants that come up from the ground.

**fountain** a large stream or flow of water coming up from the earth.

**fowl** a bird or birds; any kind of bird.

**frankincense** a sweet-smelling substance that comes from certain trees, used as a perfume and in religious ceremonies.

**fro** short for *from.* See TO AND FRO.

**fruit** 1. a part of certain plants eaten as a sweet food. Apples, peaches, and pears are fruit. 2. any plant part that can be eaten as food.

**fruitful** 1. having or giving much fruit. 2. having many children.

**plump** fat in a healthy or attractive way.

**pollute** 1. to cause air or water to become dirty with waste matter. 2. to harm or ruin something by wrongdoing.

**pomegranate** a type of reddish fruit with many seeds.

**pool** in older use, any small pond or other such natural collection of water.

**potter** a person who makes pots, dishes, and other forms of pottery.

**potter's field** a name for a place where unknown people without money are buried. The potter's field in Jerusalem may have been a place where potters (pot-makers) left their pots out to dry in the sun.

**pray** 1. to communicate with God; speak to God in some way. 2. to ask that something be done; make a request.

**prayer** the act of praying; communicating with God.

**preach** to speak in public about God and religion; give a speech or talk on God.

**preparest** an older word meaning "to prepare." "Thou preparest" means "you prepare" (you make ready).

**presence** the fact of being with someone, especially someone important. To be in the *presence* of the king means to be with the king.

**priest** a person who is specially chosen or trained to perform certain religious acts; a religious leader.

**proclaim** to state publicly that something is true; make an official statement. A statement of this kind is a **proclamation**.

**profit** 1. money that is made from some kind of business dealing. 2. any kind of benefit or advantage. 3. to make a profit; gain money or some other benefit.

**prophecy** a statement about something that will come true in the future; a statement saying what the future will bring.

**prophet** 1. a person who tells about things that will happen in the future. 2. a person who brings a message from God; someone who speaks for God. 3. a person chosen or inspired by God to be a leader.

**proverb** a short and usually simple saying that contains an important truth, and that can be used as a guide for good living.

**pruning hook** a tool made up of a pole with a long blade at one end, used to cut branches from trees.

**psalm** a song or poem in praise of God; a song to or about God.

**publish** 1. to make a book available for the public to read. 2. in older use, to make something public; make known to people.

**pure** 1. not mixed with any other thing; free from anything that spoils or ruins. 2. honest and good; not evil in any way.

**pursue** to run or go after; chase.

**quail** a type of small game bird that feeds along the ground.

**rabbi** 1. in modern use, a person who has carefully studied Jewish religious law and who is qualified as the leader of a Jewish congregation. 2. in older use, a teacher of Jewish religious law. 3. **Rabbi.** a title used to refer to Jesus, meaning "Teacher" or "Master."

**ram** an adult male sheep.

**raven** a large black bird of the crow family.

**raze** to tear down or knock down a building; completely destroy a building.

**realm** the land ruled by a king; a kingdom.

**reap** to cut or pick plants for use as food; harvest a food crop, especially a grain crop such as wheat or barley.

**reaper** someone who reaps; a person who harvests grain or other food crops.

**rebel** 1. to rise up and fight against a leader or government; fight to be free of one's ruler. 2. a person who fights in this way.

**rebellion** the act of fighting against one's government or ruler; fighting for freedom from a ruler.

**rebellious** wanting or trying to rebel; fighting against one's ruler.

**rebuke** to punish or criticize a person for doing something wrong.

**refrain** to keep from doing something; not do something.

**reign** 1. to rule as a king; rule over a kingdom. 2. the time during which a king rules.

**reigneth** an older word for *reigns*. "He reigneth" means "he reigns" (he rules).

**reject** to turn away from; not accept.

**rejoice** to be very happy about something that has happened; give great thanks.

**rend** to tear something apart, especially a piece of clothing; tear into pieces.

**repent** to feel truly sorry for something one has done wrong and decide not to do it again; change away from a bad way of acting.

**restore** to bring something back to the way that it was before; return to a state of health or life.

**restoreth** an older word for *restores*. "He restoreth" means "he restores."

**resurrection** 1. the return of a dead person to life; a bringing back to life. 2. **the Resurrection.** the return of Jesus to life after his death on the cross.

**retreat** to run or move away from the enemy during battle; go back from the enemy.

297

**revenge** a wrong or harm done by someone to another person, in return for something that the other person has done earlier to him or her.

**rewardeth** an older word for *rewards*. "He rewardeth" means "he rewards."

**righteous** knowing what is right to do and acting in this way; good, honest, and fair.

**righteousness** the fact of being righteous; being good, honest, and fair.

**rod** 1. a long, thin piece of wood; a stick. 2. such a stick used to beat someone as a punishment.

**royal** having to do with a king; done by or belonging to a king.

**runneth** an older word for *runs*. "Runneth over" means "runs over" (overflows).

**sabbath** or **Sabbath** the seventh day of the week; a day off from work, set aside to rest and worship God.

**sacrifice** 1. to give something valuable to God as a sign of respect or worship, or as a way of making up for wrongdoing. The Israelites *sacrificed* farm animals such as young sheep or goats, and also bundles of newly-harvested grain. 2. the thing that is offered up to God in this way.

**saith** an older word for *says*. "Saith the Lord" means "the Lord says."

**salvation** 1. the fact of being saved; being safe from evil or danger. 2. especially, being saved from sin and from the punishments that come from sinning.

**Samaritan** a person living in or near Samaria, an ancient city in central Palestine. The Samaritans accepted some parts of the Jewish religion but not others, and they were enemies of the Jews.

**sanctuary** a building or part of a building that is set aside for worship of God; a holy place.

**save** 1. to hold on to something and keep it for later use. 2. to rescue someone from danger. 3. to keep someone from sin and the punishments of sin.

**savior** 1. a person who saves another. 2. **Savior.** a name given to Jesus.

**scarlet** a very bright red color.

**scepter** a special decorated rod or stick held or carried by a king or other ruler as a sign of royal power.

**scorn** 1. to act as if someone is not worth respect or attention; ignore or look down on a person. 2. the feeling that someone is unimportant and not worthy of respect.

**scribe** 1. a person whose job is writing things down. In earlier times before printing machines were invented, scribes made copies of books by hand. 2. in the ancient Jewish religion, a person who studied religious law and made copies of holy writings.

**scripture** 1. a book of holy writing; a book about God. 2. see SCRIPTURE.

**Scripture** or **Scriptures** the writings of the Old Testament or the New Testament; the Bible.

**sea** 1. a large body of salt water; an ocean. 2. a large body of fresh water, such as the Sea of Galilee.

**sermon** a talk or speech given on religion and on the right way of acting according to religion.

**serpent** a snake, especially a poisonous snake.

**servant** 1. a person who lives in the house of another and is paid by the person to do household work, such as cooking or washing. 2. any person who serves another.

**shall** another word for *will*. "You shall make it in this way" means "you will make it in this way" or "you should make it in this way."

**shalt** an older word for *shall*. "Thou shalt not steal" means "you shall not steal."

**sheaves** large pieces of grain or other plants that have been gathered together in a bundle.

**shekel** 1. a small unit of weight used in ancient times; one pound is about 30 shekels. 2. a gold or silver coin having the weight of one shekel.

**shepherd** a person who takes care of a flock of sheep. Jesus is often compared to a shepherd watching over his flock.

**shield** a large, heavy piece of wood or metal. In ancient times warriors held up shields as they fought in battle to protect themselves against enemy arrows, swords, and so on.

**shield-bearer** a person who carried a warrior's shield to the battlefield.

**sickly** not healthy; sick or likely to become sick.

**sin** something that it is very wrong to do; something that is against the laws of God or that does not follow the word of God.

**sinful** filled with sin; doing wrong against the laws of God.

**sinner** a person who sins; someone who breaks the laws of God.

**slain** an older word meaning "killed."

**slaughter** the killing of a great many; the death of many people or animals at one time.

**slave** a person who is held prisoner by another and forced to work for that person without any pay. In ancient times, people who lost a war were often forced to become the slaves of the winning side.

**slavery** the fact of being a slave; being forced to work for another without pay.

**slay** an older word meaning "to kill."

298

**sling** or **slingshot**  a simple weapon used to throw a stone through the air at a high speed. The thrower spins the sling quickly overhead and then lets go of one end to make the stone fly out.

**slumber**  to be in a deep, sound sleep.

**smite**  to hit hard. To *smite* someone means to hit the person with the fist or with a weapon.

**soothsayer**  a person who claims to be able to tell what will happen in the future, by studying such signs as the flight of birds.

**sow**  to plant seeds in the ground or scatter them on the ground, so that plants will grow.

**spare**  **1.** to not use something; be able to do without something. **2.** to not kill or harm a person who is under one's power.

**spell**  a magic power that can cause something strange or amazing to happen.

**spice**  something that is added to food to make it taste better. Pepper and cinnamon are spices.

**spin**  to draw out and twist fibers to form thread or yarn for making clothing.

**spokesman**  a person who speaks for someone else, especially someone who speaks for a leader.

**stabilized**  made stable; made so that it will not move off its position or course.

**staff**  a long, thin stick or pole, somewhat like a modern broomstick.

**stank**  an older word meaning "smelled bad."

**stature**  the way a person stands. A person of great *stature* is very tall.

**statute**  a rule or law.

**stiff-necked**  not willing to give in or obey; stubborn.

**strike**  to hit hard; hit with the fist or a weapon.

**stud**  a small knob or head that stands out on the surface of something.

**stumbling block**  an obstacle or block in a person's path that the person might trip over.

**suckling**  a baby, or a pig or other such animal, that is still so young that it feeds by sucking its mother's milk rather than eating solid food.

**swaddling clothes**  in earlier times, long bands of cloth that were wrapped around a new baby just after its birth.

**swear**  **1.** to say in a very serious way that one will do something or that something is true. **2.** especially, to make a promise to God to do something. **3.** to use bad or foul language; curse.

**swine**  another name for a pig or hog.

**swore**  a past tense form of SWEAR.

**synagogue**  a place of worship for the Jewish religion.

**tabernacle**  a holy place set aside for the worship of God.

**tablet**  a flat, smooth piece of stone, used in early times for writing in the way that paper is used today.

**taketh**  an older word meaning *takes.* "He taketh away" means "he takes away."

**talent**  **1.** in modern use, the ability or skill to do something well. **2.** in ancient times, a heavy unit of weight, or a large unit of money based on this weight.

**temple**  **1.** a building used for the worship of God. **2. Temple.** a special building of this type in Jerusalem. Several different Temples were built at different times in history.

**tempt**  to try to get someone to do a bad thing; influence or persuade a person to do wrong.

**temptation**  the fact of being tempted; being influenced to do wrong.

**tend**  to take care of. To *tend* sheep means to take care of them.

**test**  **1.** a set of questions used to find out how much a student has learned. **2.** a difficult task used to find out what a person knows or believes.

**testament**  a statement that something is true or real.

**testimony**  **1.** a statement by a witness in court as to what he or she knows to be true about the case on trial. **2.** any such statement about what is true.

**thankful**  glad that something happened; giving thanks.

**thee**  an older form of the word *you.* "I have told thee" means "I have told you."

**thereof**  of or from that. "He went to the river and drank the water thereof" means "He went to the river and drank the water from it."

**therewith**  with that. "A heavy rain came, and strong winds therewith" means "A heavy rain came, and strong winds with it."

**thine**  an older form of the word *your.* "In thine house" means "in your house."

**thou**  an older form of the word *you.* "Thou has made him" means "you have made him."

**thresh**  to separate grain from the plant on which it grows, so that it can be used for food.

**thy**  an older form of the word *your.* "Thy father and mother" means "your father and mother."

**thyself**  an older form of the word *yourself.* "Do this thyself" means "do this yourself."

**to and fro**  here and there; from one place to another.

**token**  **1.** a small metal disk used in place of a coin, as in a machine. **2.** an object or sign that stands for something.

**tomb**  a building, room, or other place used to bury the dead.

**train** in older use, a long line of people traveling together on horses, camels, or other animals.

**transfigure** to change in appearance or physical form; change completely.

**tremble** to move quickly back and forth; shake, especially from fear.

**tribe** a number of people who form a single group under one leader. The members of a tribe all relate their families to one common ancestor. The Levites were a tribe descended from Levi, the son of Jacob.

**triumph** to win a battle or contest; be the winner.

**turtle** see TURTLEDOVE.

**turtledove** a type of dove, a bird known for its soft, cooing song. The phrase "the voice of the *turtle*" in the Song of Songs refers to the singing of this bird.

**unclean** 1. not clean; dirty. 2. not acceptable to God; against the rules of God. Jewish law has declared certain foods to be unclean, such as pork or shellfish.

**unleavened bread** a special type of bread that does not rise when it is baked and looks like a flat, thin cracker.

**unto** an older word for *to*. "Do unto others" means "do to others."

**upright** 1. standing straight up; vertical. 2. having a strong and honest character; being an honorable person.

**utter** to say something; speak out loud.

**vain** 1. having no value or purpose; worthless or empty. 2. **in vain.** for no reason or for the wrong reason. "To take the Lord's name in vain" means to use the name of God in the wrong way, as in cursing someone.

**vanities** things that have no effect or value; useless things.

**vanity** something that has no value or purpose; an action that does not do anything useful.

**venison** 1. in modern use, the meat of a deer. 2. in older use, the meat of any wild animal.

**vessel** 1. a boat or ship. 2. a cup or glass used to drink from.

**vineyard** a place where grape vines are grown, especially for making wine.

**virgin** a woman who has never had sex with a man.

**vision** 1. the power to see, or a thing that a person sees. 2. something a person sees that is not like an ordinary sight, such as the appearance of a dead person or an angel.

**visiteth** an older word for *visits*. "He visiteth" means "he visits."

**void** having nothing in it; without anything; empty.

**vow** 1. a very serious promise to do something. 2. to make such a promise.

**wages** payment that is made to a person for work done.

**want** 1. to be interested in getting or doing something. 2. in older use, to be without something one needs or should have.

**wanting** not having; being without; lacking.

**wayside** the side of a road or path.

**weaned** of a young child or young animal, no longer feeding on its mother's milk, but eating solid food instead.

**weep** to cry; shed tears. To say that someone *wept* means that the person cried.

**wept** see WEEP.

**whence** from what place. "From whence you came" means "from where you came."

**wherewith** an older word that means "with which."

**whirlwind** a strong wind that spins around in a circle.

**whosoever** whoever; whichever person.

**wicked** very bad; evil.

**wickedness** the fact of being very bad; being evil.

**wilderness** a wild place away from where people live; a forest, desert, or wasteland.

**wisdom** the fact of being wise; knowing a great deal.

**wither** of a plant, to dry up and die.

**witness** 1. a person who tells in a court of law what he or she has seen or knows about the case on trial. 2. a person who tells others what he or she has seen or knows. 3. to tell something in this way. The followers of Jesus witnessed to other people about his life and thoughts. 4. **false witness.** a lie or untrue statement by a person about what he or she knows or has seen.

**woe** bad luck or evil; a bad thing that happens.

**womb** the part within a woman's body in which a baby develops before it is born.

**word** 1. a sound or group of letters that has a separate meaning. 2. a message or statement from God.

**worship** to give honor to God; show one's love and respect for God.

**wrath** great anger; the fact of being very angry about something.

**ye** an older word for *you*. "Ye shall seek the truth" means "You shall seek the truth."

**yea** an older word for *yes*.

**yearn** to want something very much.

**youth** 1. the time of being young. 2. a young person, especially a young boy.

**zealot** a person who believes very strongly in some person or idea.